P9-AQX-760

WITHDRAWN

Old English Literature

By the same author

Lady Godiva: A Literary History of the Legend

Also available from Blackwell Publishing

Introduction to Old English
Peter S. Baker

A History of Old English Literature
Robert D. Fulk & Christopher M. Cain

The Blackwell Encyclopaedia of Anglo-Saxon England
Edited by Michael Lapidge, John Blair, Simon Keynes & Donald Scragg

A Guide to Old English
Sixth Edition
Bruce Mitchell & Fred C. Robinson

An Invitation to Old English and Anglo-Saxon England
Bruce Mitchell

Old Norse-Icelandic Literature: A Short Introduction
Heather O'Donoghue

A Companion to Anglo-Saxon Literature
Edited by Phillip Pulsiano & Elaine M. Treharne

Old and Middle English c.890–c.1400: An Anthology
Second Edition
Edited by Elaine M. Treharne

Old and Middle English Poetry
Edited by Elaine M. Treharne & Duncan Wu

Old English Literature

A Short Introduction

Daniel Donoghue

Blackwell
Publishing

350 Main Street, Malden, MA 02148-5020, USA
108 Cowley Road, Oxford OX4 1JF, UK
550 Swanston Street, Carlton, Victoria 3053, Australia

First published 2004 by Blackwell Publishing Ltd

Library of Congress Cataloging-in-Publication Data

Donoghue, Daniel, 1956–
Old English literature : a short introduction / Daniel Donoghue.
p. cm. — (Blackwell introductions to literature)
Includes bibliographical references (p.) and index.
ISBN 0-631-23485-3 (hardcover : alk. paper) — ISBN 0-631-23486-1
(pbk. : alk. paper)
1. English literature—Old English, ca. 450–1100—History and
criticism. I. Title. II. Series.

PR173.D66   2004
829'.09—dc22
2003018469

A catalogue record for this title is available from the
British Library.

Set in 10/13pt Meridian
by Graphicraft Limited, Hong Kong
Printed and bound in the United Kingdom
by TJ International Ltd, Padstow, Cornwall

For further information on
Blackwell Publishing, visit our website:
http://www.blackwellpublishing.com

to my mentors

Contents

Illustrations

Introduction

The Anglo-Saxons left us accounts of two defining moments in the formative years of their literature. The first is a famous story about an illiterate peasant who one night miraculously refashioned his native poetic tradition. The story is told by Bede (c.673–735), a monk who near the end of his scholarly career compiled a narrative history of the Christian church in England up to his time. The history devotes an entire chapter to the cowherd Cædmon largely because his new poetic skills were applied only to Christian stories and not because he received the gift of poetry. English poetry itself was nothing new and scarcely worth Bede's attention. For centuries before Cædmon the Anglo-Saxons had cultivated a tradition of oral poetry, which continued to celebrate its pagan themes and legends well after the conversion to Christianity. For Bede, the importance of Cædmon's innovation was that it baptized the old vernacular poetry.

For literary history, however, the story's importance lies elsewhere. Soon after receiving his God-given skills Cædmon took vows and entered the monastery, where he continued to learn sacred stories and turn them into poems. His passage from the outside world into the cloister meant that English poetry itself found a place in the monastic life, since verse-making was the only skill Cædmon could offer to the community. Before Cædmon entered, the old poetry was limited to an oral context; afterwards, it could find its way into the scriptorium. Without writing a word Cædmon opened up the possibility of English literature.

The second account is a letter from King Alfred of Wessex (871–99), which urges an ambitious program of translating certain Latin texts that were, as he put it, most necessary for all people to know. Before Alfred there was little in the way of English prose, but his efforts generated an industry that by the time of his death had produced an impressive body of literature and fixed the conventions of the emerging genre. Alfred did more than issue directives to writers, however, because he set himself to the task of translating three scholarly books and fifty psalms from Latin to English.

This book introduces students and general readers to the English literature produced in the centuries before the year 1100 CE. Today the language of this period is generally called Old English to distinguish it from Middle English (1100–1500) and Modern English (1500-present), but its speakers called it simply English. The different accounts left by Bede and Alfred, discussed more fully in the following chapters, are not quite myths of origin, but each offers a richly suggestive description of early conditions for one of the two major literary genres: verse (Bede) and prose (Alfred). Both writers, moreover, show the literature emerging from the backdrop of the Latin culture of the church. Like almost everything else he wrote, Bede narrated the story of Cædmon in Latin, which was the universal language of scholarship and an essential part of monastic life, so his validation of the vernacular carries special weight. Latin is just as much a part of the context of King Alfred's program, in which almost all the new English texts were translations.

In the relative scale of cultural prestige, English was always the poor stepchild of Latin. But unlike the status of English in later generations, when writers like William Caxton (d. 1491) felt compelled to apologize for their "rude" and "base" language, that of Old English was not so low as to be debilitating. After a theologian with the credentials of Bede gave his blessings to the poetry, and after the greatest king of early England translated the word of God, later writers were free to work in the vernacular without special pleading. One measure of the relative status of English comes in a later century, when Ælfric (c.945–c.1010), a monk, scholar, homilist, and gifted prose stylist, used the vernacular to compose a Latin grammar for use in the monastery. (It took almost another five centuries before the next English-to-Latin grammar was written.) For Ælfric Latin was unquestionably the superior language and essential to the monastic life, but English provided an adequate vehicle for teaching it.

Bede, Alfred, and Ælfric lived in three distinct eras within the larger period of pre-Conquest or Anglo-Saxon England. At its outer limits the period extends over six centuries – an interval equivalent to that between today and Chaucer's lifetime – and over those centuries the society (or rather societies) underwent enormous changes. The Anglo-Saxons themselves traced their ancestors' arrival to the year 449, when legend has it that two brothers, Hengest and Horsa, came as leaders of mercenary armies from the continent and later decided to turn on their British employers and take the land for themselves. The Angles, Saxons, and Jutes brought their pagan religion to their new home, and it was not until shortly before 600 that conversion to Christianity began, first by Irish missionaries in Northumbria and then by a special mission in the south sent by Pope Gregory the Great. Conversion proceeded gradually with some setbacks during much of the seventh century, but even by the 650s monasteries such as Whitby (Cædmon) and Jarrow (Bede) were thriving. Throughout the earlier centuries the Anglo-Saxons were politically divided into smaller, often competing kingdoms until about 800, when the four great kingdoms of Northumbria, Mercia, East Anglia, and Wessex emerged.

In 793 a raiding party of Vikings attacked the island monastery of Lindisfarne off the coast of Northumbria. It was the start of 100 years of Viking attacks, which evolved from small raids eventually to large invading armies that conquered and occupied more and more territory until the 870s, when only Wessex remained of the four kingdoms. King Alfred managed to stop the Viking advances, and eventually he and his successors won back enough territory to create a united kingdom of England, ruled by the kings of Wessex.

Alfred also instituted a program of cultural revival that indirectly led to the great Benedictine reform of the latter half of the tenth century, which produced outstanding churchmen like Archbishop Wulfstan and Abbot Ælfric. It was the period when most of the surviving manuscript volumes of Old English prose and poetry were transcribed. But the tenth century also witnessed a second wave of Viking attacks, much of it during the long and unhappy reign of Æthelred (978–1016), who was finally succeeded by the king of Denmark, Cnut (1016–35). Cnut's long reign was followed by the even longer one of Edward the Confessor (1042–66), who died childless, leaving several powerful claimants ready to pounce on the throne. First Harold

Godwineson was crowned, but in October of 1066 his rival Duke William of Normandy defeated him in the battle of Hastings, and the throne of England passed into Norman hands. The linguistic changes that distinguish Middle English from Old English would have proceeded whether or not William became king. And so to decouple linguistic change from a change of political regime scholars prefer to consider 1100 as the approximate end of Old English.

Most surveys like this one organize their material by some combination of the standard literary categories of genre, date, and/or author. But Old English quickly frustrates such schemes. The Anglo-Saxons themselves, for example, recognized histories, saints' lives, and homilies as genres because they had well-established Latin precedents, but beyond these the categories become uncertain. We do not know, for example, whether they distinguished a long poem like *Beowulf* as an "epic" as opposed to a shorter "lyric," however familiar these genres seem to us. Even categories as broad as "fiction" and "non-fiction" would probably seem strange (though not incomprehensible) to a medieval audience. The question of authorship is no less vexed. All but a few of the Old English poems are anonymous, and while a number of prose texts come to us with their authors' names, a significant number are anonymous, and still others attributed to a known author like Ælfric were not in fact written by him. The same uncertainty applies to chronology, again with more questions surrounding the poetry than the prose. We are on firmer ground in considering Old English literature through the context of the surviving manuscripts, because many of them can be placed and dated with some confidence. Each manuscript volume, moreover, generates its own micro-context in the selection and arrangement of texts that comprise it. Manuscript origin thus provides one feasible means for organizing a survey, but it presents its own set of problems, often of a technical nature.

In place of the familiar categories from literary history the following chapters organize the material into what I call "figures": the vow, the hall, the miracle, the pulpit, and the scholar. Though not drawn from any school of criticism, they would be recognizable to medieval as well as modern readers. Organizing the material this way allows a good deal of flexibility and the chance to associate texts that, if sorted by genre or date or author, might be kept separate. At the most basic level, it allows the grouping of prose and verse, the obscure and the well known, early and late periods, and even the vernacular and Latin. While each work of Old English discussed will have a "home" in one chapter (or two in the case of *Beowulf*), it may appear for brief discussion elsewhere. The figures do not designate mutually exclusive categories; some could even expand to absorb all the others. There is something arbitrary about their choice and sequence, yet cumulatively they assume a coherent shape as the literature is explored.

My use of "figure" deliberately echoes the term applied to the widespread practice of figural interpretation in the Middle Ages, which in its most basic form moves from an event or character from the Old Testament to find its fulfillment in Christ. But figural readings became generalized as a way of finding transcendental significance in many kinds of discourse, including history and fiction. This book will not make transcendental claims, but it does share with the medieval *figura* a way of pointing from a specific example to its realization in a more comprehensive scheme. My use of figures also finds a parallel in what a theorist has observed about organizing material in archives: "they are grouped together in distinct figures, composed in accordance with multiple relations, maintained or blurred in accordance with specified regularities."[1] Old English literature presents a large and diverse archive of texts that does not lend itself to cleanly defined, exhaustive categories. My use of the vow, the hall, the miracle, the pulpit, and the scholar allows me to explore the multiple relations among the texts under discussion without claiming an overarching (or transcendental) order. In fact the arbitrariness of the figures in this book becomes even more apparent when with a little effort one can spin them off in Borgesian profusion: the sea, the wound, exile, the gift, counsel, the book, the stranger, prophecy, the exchange, the hand, the hoard. Any or all of these figures could make "specified regularities" for organizing the archive.

My approach is idiosyncratic, a distillation of ideas from studying and teaching Old English for 20 years. At times the book advances new interpretations, but in most cases the discussion is informed by the received wisdom of many generations of scholars, which is often too diffuse to be pinned down, although my debt is no less real. At every turn I have been reminded of the influence of my early mentors. Even though the chapters are not organized by chronology or genre, my method of reading combines historical context with close textual analysis. The discussions seldom dwell on the manuscript context, which is quite often ably covered in the relevant editions. It also has little to say about the specifics of literary features such as poetic meter and kennings, for which a good knowledge of the language is necessary.

The book has little to say about these and other technical subjects because its intended audience is students taking introductory Old English classes, students reading the texts in translation, and general readers with an interest in the subject. I cite works using my own translations, often accompanying quotations from the original Old English. The book's system of citing Old English texts needs some explanation. With few exceptions the quotations are drawn from the classroom editions that beginning students are most likely to be using and not from scholarly editions, as is usually the case. When poetry is quoted, the passage is identified by an abbreviated name of the edition, followed by line numbers, but because the poems cited here have standard lineation any edition can be consulted. For prose, the first citation gives the abbreviated name of the edition followed by a page number and line number.

The first of the two following tables of abbreviations gives a short list of the standard classroom editions currently available for introductory Old English courses, with the abbreviations used throughout the book. The second is an expanded listing that matches the texts discussed with the various classroom editions that contain them. (A small number of quoted texts are not found in the classroom editions; in these cases their editions are cited in a note.) The practical reason for the second table's inclusion is to help readers locate another copy of a work if the edition cited in this book is unavailable. An added benefit of the table, however, is that it shows at a glance the body of literature that the field of Old English studies today has selected to define itself. It is what our students "see" as Old English literature. It represents only a fraction of the 30,000 lines of poetry and more than ten times that amount of prose that make up the corpus of Old English literature. Many scholars working in the field today might wish to adjust the list one way or the other, but the subset gives a good idea of what Old English studies currently considers – to paraphrase King Alfred – the most necessary texts for students to know. Because the list contains what this book's users are likely to read, I have accepted it (with a few exceptions) as a practical if arbitrary means of limiting the corpus. But I am not chafing under this constraint. The list offers an ample and diverse selection of texts that are early and late, prose and poetry, fictional and historical, religious and secular, simple and rhetorically complex. My hope is that the following chapters will give students a glimpse of the imaginative richness of the earliest English literature, and that they will find those moments when the culturally familiar emerges from the strangely medieval as fascinating as I do.

Abbreviations

Classroom Editions of Old English Texts

Edition	Abbreviation	For the table below
Treharne, Elaine, ed. *Old and Middle English c.890–c.1400: An Anthology, Second Edition.* Oxford: Blackwell, 2004.	*Anthology*	A
Wilcox, Jonathan, ed. *Ælfric's Prefaces.* Durham: Durham Medieval Texts, 1994.	*Ælfric*	Æ
Mitchell, Bruce, and Fred C. Robinson, eds. *Beowulf: An Edition with Relevant Shorter Texts.* Oxford: Blackwell, 1998.	*Beowulf*	B
Pope, John C., and R. D. Fulk, eds. *Eight Old English Poems.* 3rd edn. New York: Norton, 2001.	*Eight*	E
Mitchell, Bruce, and Fred C. Robinson. *A Guide to Old English.* 6th edn. Oxford: Blackwell, 2001.	*Guide*	G
Hill, Joyce, ed. *Old English Minor Heroic Poems.* Rev. edn. Durham: University of Durham, 1994.	*Heroic*	H
Baker, Peter S. *Introduction to Old English.* Oxford: Blackwell, 2003.	*Introduction*	I
Klaeber, F., ed. *Beowulf and the Fight at Finnsburg.* 3rd edn. Boston: D. C. Heath, 1950.	Klaeber	K

Edition	Abbreviation	For the table below
Needham, G. I., ed. *Lives of Three English Saints.* Rev. edn. Exeter: University of Exeter Press, 1976.	*Lives*	L
Davis, Norman, ed. *Sweet's Anglo-Saxon Primer.* 9th edn. Oxford: Clarendon, 1970.	*Primer*	P
Whitelock, Dorothy, ed. *Sweet's Anglo-Saxon Reader, in Prose and Verse.* 15th edn. Oxford: Clarendon, 1975.	*Reader*	R
Leslie, R. F., ed. *Three Old English Elegies.* Rev. edn. Exeter: University of Exeter Press, 1988.	*Three*	T
Wrenn, Charles L., and W. Bolton, eds. *Beowulf, with the Finnesburg Fragment.* 5th edn. Exeter: University of Exeter Press, 1996.	Wrenn	W

Old English Texts Discussed in this Book

Texts (e = excerpt)	A	Æ	B	E	G	H	I	K	L	P	R	T	W
Ælfric: Homily on the Nativity of the Innocents	x										x		
Ælfric: Homily on the Parable of the Vineyard											x		
Ælfric: Life of King Oswald									x		x		
Ælfric: Life of St Æthelthryth							x		x				
Ælfric: Passion of St Edmund	x				x				x	x			
Ælfric: preface to his First Series of Catholic Homilies	x	x								x			
Ælfric: preface to Genesis			x		x								
Ælfric: preface to Grammar			x										
Ælfric: preface to Lives of Saints	x		x										
Alfred: from Boethius' Consolation of Philosophy	e				e	e					e		
Alfred: from Orosius' History						e					e		
Alfred: preface to Pastoral Care	x				x						x		
Anglo-Saxon Chronicle: Battle of Brunanburh	x			x			x						
Anglo-Saxon Chronicle: Cynewulf and Cyneheard	x				x		x				x		
Anglo-Saxon Chronicle: ninth-century entries	e									e	e		
Anglo-Saxon Chronicle: other tenth-century and later entries	e				e	e					e		
Apollonius of Tyre	x												
Battle of Maldon	x		x		x						x		
Bede: Cædmon	x		e		x	x					x		
Bede: conversion of Edwin					x					x			
Beowulf	e		x		e			x			e		x

Text								
Charter from Herefordshire								
Deor	x	x		x		x		
Dream of the Rood	x	x	x	x		x		
Elene	e		x			e		
Exodus	e							
Fates of the Apostles	x							
Finnsburh Fragment		x		x		x		x
Genesis B						e		
Husband's Message	x		x				x	
Judith	x		x	x		x	x	
Riddles from the Exeter Book	e		e			e	x	
Ruin	x		x				x	
Seafarer	x	x	x			x		
Vercelli Homily X	x							
Wanderer	x	x	x	x		x		
Widsith		x	x	x	e			
Wife's Lament	x	x	x	x		x	x	
Wulf and Eadwacer	x	x	x	x				
Wulfstan: Sermo Lupi ad Anglos	x	x	x	x		x		

1

The Vow

A leaf of an eighth-century gospel book housed in Hereford cathedral preserves a summary of a legal dispute dating from a little less than 1,000 years ago. Written in the blank space immediately after the final words of John's Gospel, it relates how six prominent officials, including Hereford's Bishop Athelstan, Thurkil the White, and Cnut's royal representative Tofi the Proud, convened a shire court in the town of Aylestone, which was attended by "all the thanes of Herefordshire" (*Reader* p. 57, lines 7–8). The shire courts were seasonal gatherings that conducted and validated various legal procedures such as the transfer of property, but they were also occasions where one citizen could lodge a formal charge against another. Such an action, if contested, would begin a legal drama in which each party would assemble supporters to take oaths affirming the reputation of the claimant or defendant. On this occasion a man named Edwin came forward and made a claim against his mother for a piece of land. Because the mother was not there to speak for herself and because Thurkil the White, who as her relative might have stepped out of his judicial role to represent her interests, knew nothing of the case, the court dispatched three thanes to Edwin's mother to inquire about her son's claim on the land. The account continues:

> And when they came to her, they asked her what was her case concerning the land that her son was claiming. Then she said that she had no land that belonged in any way to him, and she became extremely angry with her son, and called to her kinswoman, Leofflæd, the wife of Thurkil the White, and spoke to her in front of them: "Here sits my

kinswoman Leofflæd, to whom after my death I grant my land and my gold and my clothing and my garments and everything that I possess." And then she said to the thanes: "Act well like thanes and announce my message to the meeting before all the good people, and inform them to whom I have granted my land and all my possessions, and to my own son nothing at all; and ask them to be witness of this." (lines 16–28)

After the thanes returned and repeated her words to the court, Thurkil the White rose up and "asked all the thanes to grant his wife the lands which her kinswoman had granted her clear from any other claim, and they did so" (lines 31–2). Thurkil then rode to Hereford cathedral and had the account recorded in the gospel book. Because it is a relatively rare account of an actual legal proceeding it has attracted a great deal of attention. It gives a glimpse into a woman's legal rights to possess and dispose of property independently of her male relatives, and even to bequeath it to a woman outside the immediate family. It also records a fascinating human vignette, a family drama where even now, almost 1,000 years later, we can imagine the mother's fury over her son's underhanded maneuver to gain control of her property.

It is a stroke of luck that this account survives, because the Anglo-Saxon legal world was primarily an oral one, in which cases were rarely transcribed, and those few that were written down lack what we might consider basic legal conventions. Despite the existence of a fairly large corpus of written law that began to accumulate as early as *c.*600 CE, no legal decision in all the centuries of Anglo-Saxon England cites or quotes an existing statute.[1] Apparently, the law codes were not applied to specific cases. Instead they had a more symbolic function. Aside from some ecclesiastical centers that preserved charters and other documents out of self-interest, there were no public archives to file away legal documents. It may seem surprising to us today that something as ephemeral as a spoken utterance, even one made with elaborate formalities in front of witnesses, would serve to affirm and publicize a legal transaction. We owe the Herefordshire account's survival to the unusual efforts made by Thurkil to put it in writing and his choice to use a book that stood a good chance of surviving the centuries because of its sacred content. (The gospel book remains in the Hereford cathedral library to this day.) If Thurkil chose to write on almost anything else, it likely would have disappeared in the intervening years. Whether it survived or not, however, his summary

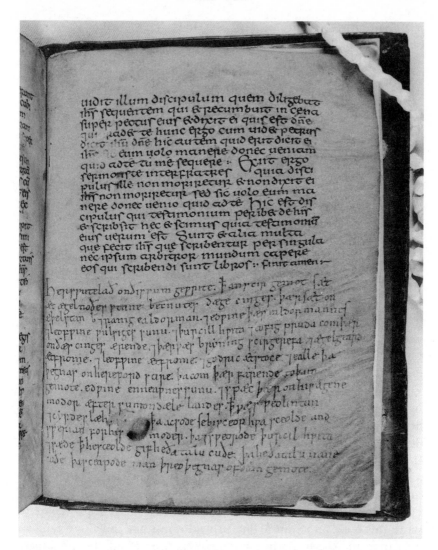

A charter from early eleventh-century Herefordshire copied after the end of the Gospel of John in the Hereford Gospel Book. Note the difference in the writing between the eighth-century Latin (insular majuscule) and below it the eleventh-century Old English (Anglo-Saxon minuscule). Hereford Gospel Book, Cathedral P.i.2, from Hereford Cathedral Library.

itself had no legal status; it could only have functioned as a reminder of the transaction confirmed by the shire court.

Thurkil's account, in fact, refers to not one but three legal transactions. The first is Edwin's original suit against his mother, which the court presumably dismissed in the end. In any case the written record has nothing more to say about it. The second is the woman's declaration in front of the three thanes that after her death her possessions will go to Leofflæd. This private declaration might have been enough for most personal wills, but to secure her decision, she enjoins the men to "act well like thanes" (*Doð þegnlice and wel*) and to petition the shire court to add their collective witness on her behalf. The court then ratifies her will, which becomes the third transaction. The additional steps taken by Thurkil and Leofflæd's kinswoman hint of a lingering worry that her son Edwin might later try more devious means to gain control of the land. Thus she asks the court to ratify her will when "all the thanes of Herefordshire" are there to witness it, and thus Thurkil takes the otherwise superfluous step of writing it down.

The primacy of the oral utterance is reflected even in the very wording of Thurkil's account, which quotes the woman verbatim: "'Here sits my kinswoman Leofflæd, to whom after my death I grant . . .'" (line 21). The use of direct speech emphasizes the crucial importance of her exact words, uttered in front of witnesses. It reminds us today that the oral culture of Anglo-Saxon England valued and depended upon the precise memory of spoken words to a far greater degree than today's more literate culture. Modern Western societies tend to think of literacy as superior and consider its privileged state as a measure of civilization. Especially in legalistic matters written documents have a primacy: "Put it in writing!" is a call for accountability. Literacy does bring many advantages, to be sure, such as my ability to write this book and your ability to read it at some indefinite remove over time and space. Yet just as Anglo-Saxon England, though largely an oral culture, made use of literacy, modern societies still depend to an impressive degree on oral utterances, as will be discussed below. And more to the point, oral societies have their own complexities and subtleties, which can take some effort for us to comprehend.

This chapter explores how formal utterances function as both a theme and at times a condition for the very existence of Old English literature. It will focus on vows such as a hero's boast or a lover's promise as particularly potent instances of what has come to be called a speech act. There is a danger, however, of overidealizing Anglo-Saxon speech acts as we reconstruct them from oblique historical references and imaginative literature. The account of the family dispute in Herefordshire, for example, seems like a resounding legal victory for the woman in question. But was she or Thurkil manipulating the system? Did she really have a better claim to the land than her son? We cannot know. Even assuming her claim was valid it is curious and a little disquieting that the written account never mentions her name. It may be an oversight, especially if Thurkil had it entered in some haste, but if so the oversight itself reminds us that women, even those with enough status and wealth to dispose of property, were still second-class citizens in Anglo-Saxon England. No women seem to be present at the shire meeting if we take the "thanes of Herefordshire" literally, yet Leofflæd and her kinswoman were apparently nearby, close enough for the three thanes to complete their round trip while the court was still in session. Moreover, within a few years of this date the land in question is listed as belonging to the clergy of Hereford and to Thurkil, not his wife Leofflæd.[2] Even stripped of any lingering nostalgic idealization, however, the Herefordshire account dramatizes how Anglo-Saxon society depended on the efficacy of the spoken word.

Writing a short time before the events in Herefordshire, Archbishop Wulfstan (d. 1023), the leading statesman and legislator of his day, circulated a homily to be read throughout England. Known by its Latin name, *Sermo Lupi ad Anglos*, or "The Sermon of Wolf to the English," it was composed in the rhythmic cadences that we still associate with oral delivery in English. For most of its length it itemizes the outrages that the Anglo-Saxons have perpetrated at every level of society, which God has punished by allowing the invading Vikings to inflict even worse crimes on them. The crimes include various kinds of violence such as murder, rape, mutilation, the desecration of churches, and enslavement, as will be discussed in a later chapter. But Wulfstan singles out for special execration a specific class of non-violent crimes: failing to keep one's word. "Also we know well," he thunders in one passage,

> where that wretched deed has happened that a father has sold his son for a price, and a son his mother, and one brother has sold another into the control of foreigners. And all these are great and terrible deeds, let him understand who will. And yet what harms this people is still greater

and even more manifold [*mare and eac mænigfealdre*]: many are forsworn and greatly perjured [*forsworene and swyðe forlogene*], and pledges [*wed*] are broken again and again. (*Reader* p. 89, lines 88–94)

As horrible as it is for one family member to sell another into slavery, what cuts even deeper into the fabric of society is the widespread loss of trust in the spoken word. If forced today to rank the two kinds of crimes, we would be more outraged at the enslavement of family, which strikes us as a betrayal of the most basic values. The breaking of pledges seems distinctly less horrible, even trivial in today's more cynical age where public officials can "retract" promises in response to focus groups and news cycles. What is a broken pledge, we might ask, in comparison with handing mom and dad over to slave traders? Yet to Wulfstan the bond of the spoken word was the *only* glue that held society together. His *Sermo* ends with several exhortations to "keep carefully oath and pledge [*að and wed*], and have some loyalty [*getrywða*] between us without deceit."[3]

Wulfstan's slightly older contemporary, the abbot and homilist Ælfric of Eynsham (*c*.945–*c*.1010), expresses quite similar sentiments in an unfinished letter concerning the responsibilities of King Æthelred's subjects to defend the kingdom. Defending Æthelred (978–1016) from criticism that he did not personally lead the English armies into battle, Ælfric compiles examples from history to show how successful kings have delegated military authority to their generals. But the letter ends in mid-argument at a passage poised to turn in a new direction urging its audience to keep fidelity to the spoken word. Ælfric plays off the closeness in sound and meaning of the noun *behat* ("promise, vow") and the verb *behatan* to make a point about the sacredness of vows: *we sceolon . . . on eornost sprecan, þæt ure behat beon þe we behatað Gode fæste and getreowe, trumran þonne stanweall.* It is worthwhile to translate the larger passage from which this excerpt is taken:

Our guidance and our defense must be from God, and we must seek from God himself our counsel with resolute mind, and speak earnestly so that our vows [*behat*] that we vow [*behatað*] to God will be firm and true [*getreowe*], stronger than a stone wall, because God is truth, and he loves truth, and he completely destroys those who speak lies just as it stands written in these Latin words: *"Thou wilt destroy all that speak a lie."*[4]

The message seems to be not that God helps those who help themselves, but that God helps those who speak the truth (*soð-fæstnyss*) and keep their word. This sentiment is quite close to Wulfstan's although couched in less alarmist language. The implication, even in the letter's unfinished state, is that while Æthelred may be justified in delegating power to his generals, they need to live up to their pledges to support him.

Beginning with the passages from Wulfstan and Ælfric, we can collect a group of Old English words that become a focal point of anxiety about the efficacy of the spoken word, including *að* "oath," *wedd* "pledge," *wær* "treaty, pledge," *treowe* "truth, promise, fidelity," and the group of related words *hatan, behatan, behat*, all three of which concern a vow or promise. These last three are in turn related to *beot* (a contraction of an earlier form of *be-hat*), which along with *gielp* assumes a prominence as the "heroic boast" in poems like *Beowulf* and *The Battle of Maldon*. But keeping one's word is not just a job for legendary heroes or Ælfric's generals. In other kinds of literature and in Anglo-Saxon society as a whole it becomes a measure of *treowþ* or "troth, good faith, fidelity." It makes the Herefordshire woman's will, the laws, and every other social transaction feasible, from commercial deals to marriage vows, from pledges of political fealty to the clergy's religious vows, from solemn liturgical ceremonies to magical charms (even if churchmen like Wulfstan and Ælfric would never countenance such superstitions).

Such uses of spoken language have come to be categorized as speech acts, in which the uttering of a sentence changes a social relation (for example, "I promise") or personal state (for example, "I believe"). In other words, the saying of something is doing something. Grammatically, the typical speech act uses first person, present tense forms of a verb, although these features are sometimes disguised by constructions that phrase it indirectly. They cannot be said to convey information, at least the kind of information that is susceptible to truth claims. While the Anglo-Saxons had an extensive working knowledge of speech acts, we have no evidence that they ever theorized about them as a special class of language, but they did consider the complications that can arise. Wulfstan's *Sermo* suggests this question: what happens when people break their promises repeatedly? In other words, what happens when someone loses his or her *treowe*?

Even if the spoken utterance preserves the form of the speech act, it might not be received as one by the audience. To use an obvious example, there is no doubt that after a couple exchanges their vows in a *weddung*, "pledge, betrothal," they conduct themselves as if their social relation has changed, and indeed the rest of society treats the newlyweds as a new entity. Most modern Western societies lack a corresponding ceremony to *dissolve* a marriage by means of a speech act; that is, "I hereby declare myself divorced from you." While an early Anglo-Saxon penitential, for instance, allows a woman to repudiate her husband for impotence, it is not clear if she does so orally in front of witnesses. On the other hand the sagas of medieval Iceland dramatize a number of divorces by speech act. In *Njal's Saga*, for example, Thrain Sigfusson impulsively names witnesses and declares himself divorced from his sharp-tongued wife Thorhild after she lampoons him with verse. It takes place during the feast celebrating the wedding of Gunnar Hamundarson and Hallgerd Hoskuldsdottir, where Thrain has been eyeing the bride's beautiful daughter Thorgerd. Thrain's ogling enrages his wife Thorhild, who improvises a couplet to humiliate him in front of the wedding guests: "This gaping is not good, / Your eyes are all agog." After his impulsive divorce, Thrain just as impulsively asks for Thorgerd's hand. "I don't know about that," says her grandfather Hoskuld. "It seems to me that you have barely parted from the one you had before."[5] Nevertheless Thrain's proposal is accepted, and the wedding turns into a double ceremony. The story is worth contemplating because it highlights the way that society must sanction each speech act (here a divorce or a wedding). Afterwards individuals have to receive it as valid and conduct themselves accordingly. (In the example from *Njal's Saga* the divorced Thorhild seems to have no recourse: she is no longer married to Thrain.) Ælfric's and Wulfstan's anxiety is not the disappearance of pledges and oaths but their widespread untrustworthiness. The two seem to sense an imminent threat that, once it is compromised too far, the whole network of social bonds will collapse on itself.

The Herefordshire woman's orally declared will before three thanes is a clear instance of a speech act, the core of which is "I grant" and which she enjoins the thanes to repeat word for word to the shire court. Her language thus assumes a substantial form, not in any material sense, but as a linguistic formulation retained in memory and reproduced publicly as an utterance. It is possible to see law as well as countless other activities of Anglo-Saxon society conducted through a vast network sustained by individual memory and oral performance. Because the spoken word is by nature ephemeral, it is impossible to tell with certainty how the Anglo-Saxons used speech acts, but the imaginative literature they left contains a number of instances, which form the focus of the remainder of this chapter.

Wulf and Eadwacer is one of the most enigmatic yet emotionally compelling lyrics in Old English. Its narrow focus on the speaker's affective response allows only a hint of the larger narrative context, which is very likely a legend once widely known but now lost. A prevalent interpretation holds that the speaker's lover is a man named Wulf, from whom she has been separated by her marriage to Eadwacer. The two men are enemies. The speaker's words constitute a fictional speech act against the man who has married her against her will, but the textual ambiguities remain so pervasive that any reading must be tentative. The ambiguity begins with the first three lines. One possible translation is, "It is for my people as if one gives them a gift [*lac*]. They will serve him [food] if he comes into the company. It is different for us" (*Guide* lines 1–3). Who are her "people"? Who are "us"? And in what way is "it" different? The translation offered here adopts the more neutral or optimistic meaning of several crucial words, but the poem's tone grows increasingly dark until the sixth line reveals "there are bloodthirsty men on that island" where her lover Wulf is. Immediately the second line is repeated, *willað hy hine aþecgan gif he on þreat cymeð*, but this time the meaning of the key words becomes more threatening: "They will kill [*literally* consume] him if he comes into the armed troop" (line 7). At this point the audience – or more specifically someone imagined encountering the poem for the first time – may circle back and revise the first line's interpretation in a more ominous direction, because *lac* can mean not only "gift" but also "sacrifice": "It is as if one offers them a sacrifice." The initial ambiguity thus adds to a sense of haunting terror.

After recounting how the "battle-bold one," presumably Eadwacer, took physical possession of her, the speaker turns again to her separation from Wulf, which has made her so distraught that she declares: "Do you hear, Eadwacer? Wulf will carry our wretched whelp to the woods" (line 16). This declaration has the force of a menacing prophecy (that is, "I foretell the death of our child"). Or it could be a veiled curse; that is, an imprecation calling upon higher powers to ensure their child's destruction. In either case her words are not merely wishful thinking, but a speech act of frightening force, all the more startling because the victim will be the speaker's own child, sacrificed to satisfy an overwhelming urge for vengeance. In the final lines the *giedd* which can be "easily severed" is as polysemous as any word in the poem. Its basic meaning is "song, poem," but it can mean "riddle," "story, narrative," or "speech," and in the context of the poem's multiplying enigmas seems expandable to include any tie that binds the speaker to Eadwacer, even the *giedd* that was once their wedding vows.

Wulf and Eadwacer is one of the few poems which by itself constitutes a fictional speech act. In many more cases speech acts form an imaginative core within a larger fiction. A number of these preserve the focus on the lyrical "I," the introspective voice that articulates a subjective response to a narrative hovering just beyond the audience's reach. The first line of *The Wife's Lament* begins with *ic* ("I") and ends with *geomorre* ("sad"), the inflected ending of which alerts the reader that the speaking "I" is a woman, who relates a *giedd* about herself and her miseries (*Guide* line 1). Like the lyric "I" in *Wulf and Eadwacer*, she tells a story of loss and separation from her *hlaford*, "lord," who may be a lover or her husband. (The name commonly given to the poem, *The Wife's Lament*, is a late Victorian invention with no manuscript authority. As with every other poem discussed in this book, the manuscript gives it no name.) Unlike the other poem's "I," however, she is abandoned on an island, where she must endure her exile, *wræc-siþa*, until she can be reunited with her lord (although this part is not explicit). Her sense of loss is twofold: separation from her *hlaford* and from her homeland. While the poem's vocabulary is full of words of loss and desolation, the emotional weight of her anguish becomes focused on the bleak landscape where she must spend her days alone, where she remembers happier times and imagines lovers elsewhere sharing a bed in the early hours of the morning. While the poem nowhere says that they are married, she refers to her man as *hlaford* and *leod-fruma*, "people's leader," which is consistent with how an Anglo-Saxon wife might refer to her husband. Today our ears are also attuned to the power relation that "lord" implies, which makes it difficult to imagine an amorous relation between an inferior and a superior without the real possibility of exploitation and coercion. However, the Anglo-Saxons turned instinctively to the terms of lordship and service because they conceived those relations to be based primarily on affection. A passage from *The Wanderer* provides the best-known example: "he embraces and kisses his lord and lays hands and head on his knee" (*Guide* lines 41–2). As discordant as it may seem today, gestures of political fealty provided a basic lexicon for sexual and other kinds of friendship. In today's English-speaking world, by contrast, the language of emotional and sexual attachment has achieved a primacy, which is available for other areas of discourse to draw from. If the lovers in *The Wife's Lament* are not married, they at least have exchanged pledges in a way that modulates the hierarchy implied in *hlaford* through a kind of reciprocity signaled by the dual pronouns: "Very often we two [*wit*] promised that nothing else but death would separate us [*unc*]" (21–2). The word used for "promise," *beotedan*, is part of the word family that includes *behatan* and *beot*, which along with the dual pronouns suggests that the vows were exchanged in an equivalent way.

The Wife's Lament also contains a surprising construction of the feminine subject in a way that is remarkable, yet little remarked. The clearest instance of this begins in line 15, where the narrator starts to speak of her solitary condition and her *geomor* mind. "Then," it goes on, "I found for me a very suitable person, ill-fated, sad at heart, with a concealing mind, contemplating violence with a cheerful demeanor" (18–21). Every modern interpretation takes *monnan* "person" to refer to her lover, perhaps because the standard editions usually gloss the word as "man," which may induce readers mistakenly to assume it cannot refer to the feminine "I." But *monna*, a variant of the more familiar *mann*, primarily means "person, human being," with no reference to natural gender. The verb *funde* can mean a variety of things besides "find," including "imagine, devise, contrive," and even "invent"; and it can be used reflexively. In short the sentence can refer to the construction of her own identity: "I invented for myself a very suitable person, ill-fated, sad at heart, with a concealing mind, contemplating violence with a cheerful demeanor." As such the lyric is not only a lament but a fictional self-fashioning contrived as a woman's response to the most trying social forces. There is nothing in the lines immediately surrounding this sentence to suggest that the *monna* must be her lover/husband, and indeed the passage leading up to it concerns the woman's own condition. To what extent is the usual interpretation that masculinizes the *mod* ("mind") motivated by an unacknowledged modern reflex, a misplaced gallantry that steers violence away from the woman and forecloses the possibility of interpreting it any other way? Murderous thoughts, according to this way of thinking, are unladylike – or as monstrous as Lady Macbeth. But it does not take long to think of violent-minded counterexamples from the period, such as the feminine narrator of *Wulf and Eadwacer*. By constructing itself as the subjective experience of a fictional woman, *The Wife's Lament* not surprisingly gives the audience insight into her emotional and mental state. The same cannot be said of the *hlaford*. We learn about him primarily through the narrator's musings on his external actions: he exchanged vows with her; after the feud arose he put her in a place of safekeeping in an oak grove; then he went into exile. Indeed the only lines that refer to his subjective experience come at the end of the poem, when the narrator imagines her *wine werigmod*, "weary-hearted friend," sitting in lonely exile: "My friend suffers great anxiety; too often he remembers a happier dwelling" (50–2). Yet even this insight into his emotional state is mediated by the female subject.

The narrative transition to her lover's imagined state of mind comes immediately after a second generalization about the interior life of a *geong mon*: "A young person must always be sad-minded, hard-hearted in thought and likewise must have a happy demeanor in addition to anxiety, myriad lasting sorrows" (42–5). Most editions begin a new paragraph with these words (although there is no break in the manuscript), thus marking off the aphorism from the immediately preceding lines, which end with the narrator lamenting "all the longing which seizes me in this life" (41). The deft syntactic transition from the generalized *geong mon* passage to the specific *min freond* ("my friend") makes its application to him beyond doubt, but the aphorism's *exclusive* application to the man may derive (again) from post-medieval assumptions about what emotions are appropriate for a woman. Taken on its own, the sentiment about grief, anxiety, and a dissimulating appearance is not exclusively masculine; its applicability can extend not only to her *freond* (as it clearly does) but also to the lyric "I." Its placement between the passage describing the woman's *mod-cearu* ("heart-grief") and the later lines about her man makes it a middle term that can pivot the imaginative turn from one lover to the other. In light of the equivalence suggested in their exchanged vows, there is something appropriate about the symmetry of the lovers' suffering, even while the narrative springs from the woman's interior life.

The short lyric known as *The Husband's Message* has often been interpreted as a companion piece to *The Wife's Lament*, which precedes it by a few folios in the Exeter Book, a tenth-century manuscript compilation that contains dozens of poems. It is impossible to know whether the two were conceived as a pair or the similarities are fortuitous. However, the correspondences are striking: in both poems the woman is forced into a lonely exile, separated from her beloved because of a feud that has embroiled him. While their situation remains unresolved in *The Wife's Lament, The Husband's Message* presents itself as a welcome message carved on a rune stick (see chapter 3 for more on runes), or rather as a double message: on one level the five runic letters in the last lines of the poem convey a cryptic message, but the body of the poem is a more discursive narrative that the stick utters through a rhetorical trope in which an inanimate object is imagined to describe itself in its own voice. (The device is known as prosopopoeia; see the discussion in chapter 3.) It grew up as a species of tree, it begins, but also speaks of itself as an Anglo-Saxon retainer whom its *mon-dryhten* or "lord" has sent as an emissary to the woman: "I dare to promise [*gehatan dear*] that you will find glorious fidelity [*treowe*] there" with her partner (*Introduction* lines 11–12). It conveys the lord's request that she remember the vows (*word-beotunga*, line 15) which they once made and their *freond-scype* (19). The feud is over. He has happily returned to their homeland with treasure, horses, and the pleasures of the mead hall. There is nothing lacking in his good fortune now except her presence, so the messenger stick conveys the lord's request that she sail to him when the song of the cuckoo announces the arrival of spring.

The poem ends with a short passage incorporating the five runic letters ᚻ, ᚱ, ᛠ, ᚹ and ᛗ (*sigel, rad, ear, wynn* and *monn*), which seem to be all that the stick has carved on it, but they comprise such an enigmatic combination that their interpretation has inspired a good deal of fruitless scholarly speculation. They cannot be arranged into any pertinent word. The Old English names for the runes can be set in certain configurations as separate words or compounds, but not in a way that makes obvious sense as a message. It is more likely that the runes are the couple's predetermined code with the message "when you see these (arbitrary) runes, you will know it is safe to return home." Even though the speaking "I" identifies itself as the stick, as the poem unfolds the audience realizes that the apparent emotional depth of the stick's words comes from the woman, who imaginatively displaces her reaction onto it while she reads. Even though the runes signify little more than "come home" on the most literal level, they trigger an elaborate act of reader response in which she projects back onto the stick the painful memory of her exile. Thus the rhetorical device of giving voice to the stick imputes to the runes' opaqueness a fuller story of the couple's past ordeals and their imminent happy resolution. In the fiction imagined through the poem's narrative, the stick and the husband say everything and the woman says nothing. But in effect the entire poem is hers.

When in the poem's final lines the stick announces its five inscribed runes, it does so within the significant context of the couple's earlier speech acts:

> Concerning the old vow [*gebeot*] between you two
> I hear ᛡ together with ᚱ, ᛏ, ᛈ and ᛗ
> declare an oath [*aðe*]
> that he wished to keep the pledge [*wære*]
> and the vow of friendship [*wine-treowe*] as long as he lived
> which you two often uttered in earlier days.
>
> (49–54)

In a final twist of prosopopoeia, the stick is imagined not only speaking its message, but listening to the runes announce themselves. They orally declare (*benemnan*) themselves as witnesses who confirm by their own oath (*að*) the couple's earlier pledge. The stick expands its role from a simple messenger to a participant in a small legal drama much like that of the Herefordshire woman declaring her will before three thanes, only in this case the stick represents the man's interest and calls on the runes to swear an oath attesting to his *treowe*. While their dramatic speaking and witnessing seem like startling roles for a mute stick etched with five arbitrary letters, the poem can make this move by exploiting a pun on *treow*, a homograph for two Old English words, one of which means "tree" and the other "troth, fidelity." The overlap is not (as with other puns) a mere phonological coincidence because the two senses of *treow* share an Indo-European root meaning "to be firm, solid, steadfast." While the poet could not know of their remote linguistic history, of course, it is faintly possible that the semantic association was perpetuated through the formulaic conservatism of oral poetry. Whatever the level of awareness, however, the pun linking a tree's physical solidness to the firmness of one's good faith was available because of the identical pronunciation of the two words. The stick announces itself in the first lines as *treo-cyn* who vouches for the *treow* of the man and in the final lines conveys the man's *wine-treow* "vow of friendship." Once the punning associations are clear it is less startling that the carved etchings of a wooden *treow* are given voice as witnesses. Within the fictive world of *The Husband's Message* the stick has traveled a long distance from one lover to the other, and the final lines extend the imagined journey from the physical to the social, from writing in its most palpable form to the shared recollection of their earlier spoken vows.

The Battle of Maldon is one of the few Old English poems that can be assigned even an approximate date, because there is a general consensus it was written within decades after 991, when the battle it commemorates was fought. Although it draws on the specifics of the local geography and personal names, the poem clothes the action with literary conventions that create a general tone of nostalgia for a timeless heroic past – a past that likely never existed in any form quite resembling its conventional expression, much like the mythologized cowboys of the American West. Briefly, it tells the story of Byrhtnoth's heroic defeat in battle against an army of Vikings who had landed at the mouth of the Blackwater River (then called Pante) near the town of Maldon in south-east England. As the "ealdorman" of Essex, Byrhtnoth held one of the most powerful political positions in England after the king, and it would have fallen under his responsibilities to see to the defense of towns like Maldon. The Vikings had set up camp on an island separated by a water channel from the mainland, where Byrhtnoth summoned the local *fyrd* or militia to supplement his own personal retinue that formed the core of the defending force. After an exchange of challenges and a skirmish on the causeway connecting the island to the mainland, Byrhtnoth allowed the Vikings to cross over so that the two armies could begin a pitched battle. During the fighting, as the poem describes it, Byrhtnoth is struck down, some cowards run away, and the Vikings break through the Anglo-Saxons' "shield-wall," which ensures a disastrous defeat. The poem expends most of its rhetorical energy, however, on the heroic conduct of Byrhtnoth and his followers who chose to stay on and fight even after their army's defeat and their own death was assured.

A good deal of perceptive criticism has been written about the Anglo-Saxon heroic ethos as it is exhibited in poems like *The Battle of Maldon*. The *Germania* of the Roman historian Tacitus, completed in 98 CE, provides the starting point and the *locus classicus* for discussions of the *comitatus* (his word, meaning "retinue") and other aspects of the early Germanic military world. One memorable passage summarizes the dynamic between the chief and his followers:

> When battle has been joined, it is shameful for a leader to be surpassed in valour, shameful for his retinue to lag behind. In addition, infamy and lifelong scandal await the man who outlives his leader by retreating from the battle-line: to defend their chief and guard him, to ascribe to his glory their own brave deeds, is their foremost oath. The leaders fight for victory, the retainers for their leaders.[6]

In an obvious, commonsensical way this passage applies to the heroic efforts of Byrhtnoth and his followers in *The Battle of Maldon*, but it helps to give it some perspective by remembering that the late Anglo-Saxon world of Byrhtnoth and King Æthelred, some nine centuries after Tacitus, was far more cosmopolitan than the tribal culture found in the pages of *Germania*.

To be sure Tacitus' world of honor-bound loyalty finds analogues in earlier centuries of Anglo-Saxon England, most notably the fascinating account recorded in the *Anglo-Saxon Chronicle* for the year 755. It tells the story of a nobleman from a royal family, Cyneheard, whose brother was once the king of Wessex until a rival, Cynewulf, drove him into exile, where he was killed. Cyneheard nursed his urge for vengeance for 30 years until he found the opportunity to ambush King Cynewulf while he was visiting his concubine in the fortified town of Merton. The small raiding party killed Cynewulf after a brave solo fight, and his bodyguard, who were caught shamefully unawares, were also killed one by one as they came rushing out too late to protect their king. Before they were slain, however, Cyneheard offered each of them "treasure and life" if they would switch allegiance and follow him (*Guide* pp. 209–10, lines 19–20). They refused, preferring death with honor. A larger force loyal to the dead Cynewulf soon besieged the usurper Cyneheard within Merton. Cyneheard again offered them money and land if they would accept him as king, and besides, he added, some of your kinsmen are here with me who do not wish to leave. The besiegers say, in a classic expression, "no kinsman was dearer than [our] lord, and [we] will never follow his killer" (30–2). Nevertheless, they add, any of our kinsmen are free to leave before the fighting begins. The offer is refused. In the ensuing battle Cyneheard and all but one of his force are killed. Even though Cyneheard's ambush of Cynewulf was politically treacherous, he may have claimed an age-old legal justification to pursue the feud, and the men from both sides behaved honorably according to the ethos described by Tacitus, in which the bonds that tie a warrior to his lord are stronger than kinship and the allure of wealth.

The story of Cynewulf and Cyneheard, with its terse, breathless prose, reads like a tragically honorable exemplum that may or may not reflect the political realities of Wessex in the first half of the eighth century. But the warrior culture in *Germania* is certainly an anachronism by the end of the tenth century, when the population of England was larger, political ties were less personal, and national politics was preoccupied with insurrection from within and military threats from abroad. When King Edward the Martyr was murdered in 978 by Ealdorman Ælfhere of Mercia, the leader of a party supporting Edward's younger half-brother Æthelred, it was a raw exercise of power politics, a now-familiar *coup d'état* to install a more favorable leader. The new King Æthelred, still a boy of about 10, was a pawn in a powerful struggle between rival political factions. In this world the Germanic chiefs of Tacitus and Cyneheard's honor-bound personal loyalty were relics of a bygone past. By the late tenth century the dangers to the king were less personal though no less threatening. Something of the change can be sensed in the brief entry for 991 in the *Anglo-Saxon Chronicle*, which succinctly puts the battle at Maldon in the context of other events:

In this year Ipswich was ravaged, and very soon afterwards Ealdorman Byrhtnoth was slain at Maldon. In that year the advice was first given that payment should be made to the Danish people because of the great terror they wrought along the coast. It was initially ten thousand pounds. Archbishop Sigeric first gave that advice. (*Guide* p. 213, lines 20–4)

Here the response to the Danes is motivated not by honor but by political expediency, and in fact the policy of paying tribute was no better or worse than others proposed up to that time. Military resistance had its successes, but it could be ineffective for a number of reasons. The Vikings were formidable fighters and very mobile in their ships. If they found themselves threatened by an English army, they could simply return to their ships and sail to a more advantageous location. Notably absent in the entry for 991 is the name of King Æthelred, who after all was the one who made the decision to give 10,000 pounds of silver (an extraordinarily large sum!) to the Danes. A closer inspection of the precise Old English wording, however, shows that the king's name may not be entirely missing. *Æþel-ræd* was a fairly typical compound that literally means "noble counsel." While the *Chronicle* writer takes care to avoid naming the king, the entry contorts the syntax to use *ræd* in various forms: *And on þam geare man gerædde þæt man geald;* literally, "And in that year one counseled so that one gave." It ends *þæne ræd gerædde Siric arcebiscop,* "That advice advised Archbishop Sigeric." The awkward impersonal constructions using *man* call attention to the absence of the agent responsible for making those decisions, no matter what role Archbishop Sigeric had in the matter. The care that the chronicler takes to use the morpheme *ræd* in three words reminds his audience of the expensive and controversial "counsel" to pay off the Vikings, and the contrived repetition might suggest an ironic twist to the meaning of *Æþel-ræd.* While it might be too dangerous for a chronicler to insult the king directly, we know from later sources that Æthelred was given the nickname *Æthelræd Unræd,* an oxymoron literally meaning "noble counsel, foolish counsel." Why might a chronicler slip in an oblique criticism of the king? As a historical survey of this period summarizes, "Æthelred had one of the longest reigns in English history, 37 years (979–1016), a reign of almost unremitting disaster that has impressed itself on the folk-memory of the English."[7] These were not happy times.

The *Chronicle* entry for 991 also gives a brief mention of Byrhtnoth's death at *Mældun,* which stands in bleak contrast to the new policy of tribute to the Danes (and in contrast to the poem's fuller treatment of his death). There is little point, however, in reading his *obit* as part of the chronicler's criticism of the king, for two reasons: first, there was no choice but to note the death of someone as prominent as Ealdorman Byrhtnoth in 991, and second, his defeat in battle would support an argument in favor of the king's new policy of paying tribute. If the veteran ealdorman of Essex with a sizeable army cannot defend his own territory from the Vikings, then who can?

Such concerns of a national defense policy, however, are largely absent from *The Battle of Maldon*, the style and tone of which indulge in a poetic nostalgia for an imagined heroic world. Its focus is more local. Yet even as it celebrates the conduct of Byrhtnoth and his followers at the moment of battle, one area where the personal expands into the political is the moral imperative to live up to one's pledges. It helps to remember the exhortations of Wulfstan and Ælfric, who as clerics had a primary concern with the spiritual welfare of the people, but each felt motivated enough by events in the secular world to lament and condemn the erosion of *treowþ*. The sequence of speeches in *The Battle of Maldon*, while echoing the older ethos of loyalty to one's leader and a personal code of honor, becomes a means of addressing the same social crisis as Wulfstan's *Sermo Lupi* and Ælfric's unfinished letter addressed. Their dates of composition in the latter decades of Æthelstan's reign (respectively 1014 and after 1005) make them roughly contemporary to the presumed date of composition for *The Battle of Maldon*.

While the poem is full of memorable passages describing heroic behavior, there is an equal and often overlooked emphasis on speech acts. Because the poem survives only in an eighteenth-century copy (made shortly before the manuscript was destroyed by a fire in 1731), and because it is missing an unknown number of lines from the beginning and end, it is difficult to construct any argument about the overall structure. The first lines, abruptly picking up the middle of a scene concerning the response of (the otherwise unknown) Eadric to the summons to war, announce approvingly that "he fulfilled the boast when he was obliged to fight before his lord" (*Guide* lines 15–16). The two key words here are *gelæstan* "to fulfill, perform," and *beot*, which has been defined variously as "vow, promise, boast, vaunt," a semantic range that helps define a basic part of heroic behavior. *The Dictionary of Old English* gives it the simple definition "vow," but notes that it is disproportionately frequent in poetry and concerns especially a "formal vow of a warrior before battle."[8]

The formal challenge given by the *wicinga ar*, "Vikings' messenger," is the first overt speech act of the poem, and it is delivered *on beot*, "threateningly." The Viking's short speech is a masterpiece of cunning and backhanded diplomacy, which begins by addressing the leader Byrhtnoth using the singular pronoun *þu, þe*, then switching to the plural *ge, eow* as soon as the subject of tribute is raised.[9] It is as though the *wicinga ar* suspects that the local men who make up the *fyrd* are unsure about fighting, which he exploits by suggesting that Byrhtnoth has the most to lose by paying tribute and thus the most to gain by jeopardizing the lives of his soldiers. The messenger also switches to the all-encompassing pronoun *we, us* in the "let's be reasonable" moment of his speech, in which he laments "there is no need for us to kill each other if you succeed in [gathering tribute]," *Ne þurfe we us spillan gif ge spedaþ to þam* (34). His rhetorical strategy is to speak past the army's leader to his assembled foot-soldiers in order to break their resolve. Byrhtnoth's even more defiant reply uses the very terms of the Viking's challenge and delivers it as the *folc* speaking with a single voice:

> Gehyrst þu, sælida, hwæt þis folc segeð?
> Hi willað eow to gafole garas syllan.
> (*Guide* 45–6)

Do you hear, sailor, what this *folc* says? They wish to give you spears as tribute.

It is a challenge rolled up in vow, a speech act that Byrhtnoth extends to include everyone from himself down to the free peasants in the ranks of the *fyrd*.

After Byrhtnoth falls early in the fighting and the fortunes of war turn against the soldiers from Essex, several prominent men take flight, whom the poet is careful to name so that their disgrace will be commemorated as long as the poem survives (185–201). The point is not simply that Godric, Godwine, and Godwig ran like cowards but that they broke their promise to support their lord, who had sealed the pledge with the gift of horses (185–97). It was an outcome that Offa at a meeting before the battle had predicted: "many spoke bravely there who later had no wish to suffer in a time of need" (200–1).

Then follows a series of short speeches by men of descending rank who continue fighting even though they know that they will not survive. Ælfwine recalls how "we often spoke at mead-drinking, when in the hall we warriors on the bench raised boasts [*beot*] about hard conflict" (213–14). After proclaiming his family ancestry, he declares that he lost more than others with Byrhtnoth's death, because "he was both my kinsman and my lord" (224). After Ælfwine, Offa speaks of the need for warriors to embolden one another in battle (231–43). Next Leofsunu says, "I vow [*gehate*] that I will not flee a foot's pace but will go forward to avenge my lord [*wine-drihten*] in the conflict" (246–8). Finally Dunnere, a free peasant, gives a simple exhortation on the need to avenge one's lord without concern for life. After each speech the man goes forward to meet certain death at the hands of the Vikings.

As the fighting continues "Long Edward" (*Eadweard se langa*) speaks vaunting words (*gylp-wordum*, line 273) before he and others advance. So does Offa, who fulfilled what he had promised (*gehet*) his lord as he had vowed (*beotode*) (289–90). The most famous lines of the poem are spoken by Byrhtwold, an old retainer (*eald geneat*), who says:

> Hige sceal þe heardra,   heorte þe cenre
> mod sceal þe mare,   þe ure mægen lytlað.
> Her lið ure ealdor   eall forheawen
> god on greote.   A mæg gnornian
> se ðe nu fram þis wigplegan   wendan þenceð.
> Ic eom frod feores;   fram ic ne wille,
> ac ic me be healfe   minum hlaforde,
> be swa leofan men,   licgan þence.
>
> (312–19)

Courage must be firmer, the heart keener, spirit must be greater as our strength dwindles. Here lies our good leader entirely cut down on the dirt. He who intends to turn back now from this battle can always lament it. I am wise in years; I have no wish to leave, but I intend to lie by the side of my lord, by such a beloved man.

Byrhtwold does not call his eloquent speech a *beot*, but it does not need that self-reflexive identification to become a vow; *fram ic ne wille* is enough.

What is being celebrated in the poem? Interestingly, it is not the fighting prowess of the Anglo-Saxons. It is easy to imagine a poem recounting a similar battle where Anglo-Saxons were defeated, but only after slaying large numbers of the Danish force, or one where Byrhtnoth meets his death only after a prolonged fight with a Viking champion (like Hector fighting Achilles). However, *The Battle of Maldon* has a different agenda, in which the manner of the hero's death is more important than the killing of Vikings. Its account makes the fighting seem one-sided. Beginning with Ælfwine (209), each man's speech is followed by his return to the melee, in which the inevitability of each death seems to go beyond the ambiguous workings of fate; it is almost automatic. Ælfwine and some others have modest success in fighting, but for a poem with so many battle scenes the tally of enemy killed is slight (which is to say it may be realistic, but that is not the point). In making its heroes unexceptional fighters, the poem constructs a heroism measured by something other than a body count. It is not that the tenth-century Anglo-Saxons made poor soldiers; the historical record shows they were more than capable on the battlefield. Byrhtnoth in particular was a veteran of battles and by some accounts a tall, imposing man, but in the poem even he quickly falls victim. Soon after the fighting begins he receives a spear wound. After he kills the *ceorl* who threw it and a second Viking, he is struck down by another spear, then his arm is injured by a sword, and finally *hæðene scealcas*, "heathen warriors," finish him off (181). It is not even clear who kills him. It does not matter. Even though other sources identify the Viking leader as Olaf Trygvasson, the poem consistently presents the invaders as nameless, faceless killers, especially in the second half of the poem where their brutal efficiency gives them an almost allegorical function as agents of death.

The Battle of Brunanburh is often compared to *Maldon* because both were written shortly after the tenth-century battles they commemorate. But the differences are just as telling, beginning with the length of *Brunanburh*, which is less than one quarter that of *Maldon*, and the happier fortunes of the Anglo-Saxon army. The poem survives in four copies of the *Anglo-Saxon Chronicle* as the entire entry for the year 937, and like a good annals entry it reports the salient facts without digressive embellishment. It announces its business in the first sentence: "In this year King Athelstan, lord of noblemen, ring-giver of warriors, and also his brother prince Edmund, won endless praise with their swords in battle around Brunanburh" (*Eight* lines 58–64). The combined armies from Wessex and Mercia meet an invading force from Dublin led by the Viking King Anlaf (Olaf) and the king of the Scots and Picts, Constantine III. It is an annihilating defeat for the invaders, who (the poem tells us) leave seven earls, five kings, and Constantine's own son among the dead. In describing the carnage, the poem deploys the motif or type-scene that has come to be known as the beasts of battle, the carrion-eaters who will consume the corpses: "the dark-coated, horned-beak raven [*hræfn*], the dusky-coated white-tailed eagle [*earn*], . . . the greedy war-hawk [*guþ-hafoc*], and the gray beast, the wolf [*wulf*] in the forest" (60–5). In *The Battle of Maldon* and most other poems that use the motif, the animals materialize in anticipation of battle either before or while the armies assemble. It is as if the presence of fate (or its personification Fate) is so palpable that even wild beasts can sense it, and it thus becomes a means of testing the heroic resolve of the warriors, who know that many are destined to die. In *Maldon* the relevant lines read: "The time had come that fated persons there had to die. A shout was raised there, ravens circled, the eagle eager for carrion" (104–7).

In *Brunanburh*, however, the beasts of battle become yet another means of reckoning heroism in proportion to the carnage, in contrast to *Maldon*. But the single greatest formal difference from *Maldon* is the absence of direct speech. As with other chronicle entries, the historical distance between the narrative voice and the action it describes discourages certain literary devices such as character development and dialogue, which would be more fitting in an eye-witness account or a fictional re-creation. In any case *The Battle of Brunanburh* has no direct speech and therefore no opportunity for a speech act – that is, none except for a curious passage near the end where "books speak to us," *us secgað bec* (68), as if in a bookish environment like the *Anglo-Saxon Chronicle* the only witnesses are not humans but other written artifacts. (For a discussion of the complex transmission history of the *Chronicle*, see chapter 5.) Thus, in a personification reminiscent of the talking runes in *The Husband's Message* where a living voice is projected onto mute ciphers, the books ventriloquize a speech act attesting to the truth of the chronicle's claims.

In the large corpus of Old English literature, *Beowulf* is the work most familiar to the general public and the only one likely to be included in college and secondary school survey courses. In the scholarly world it has also been the beneficiary of more books and articles than any other text from the period, for reasons that are partly historical and partly aesthetic. Yet, as well known and studied as it is, there is surprisingly little scholarly consensus about basic matters such as authorship and the date and means of composition. For the purposes of this study I assume it to be the work of a single author who combined a deep familiarity with the Germanic oral poetic tradition with at least some training in Latin, and who flourished in the eighth century. I also consider it to be a work of breathtaking poetic brilliance, the equal of a "classic" from any period of literature. The discussion that follows examines it from two of many possible perspectives: the vow and (in the next chapter) the hall.

In recent years *Beowulf* has reached an even wider reading public with the commercial success of the poetic translation by Seamus Heaney, who in his Translator's Introduction characterizes its plot as three *agons* (or struggles) divided between the hero's youth and old age.[10] Because it is popularly known as a heroic saga or epic (a designation avoided by many Anglo-Saxonists), new readers who expect the main character to combine action-hero exploits with laconic self-expression (think of Clint Eastwood, Vin Diesel, or Arnold Schwarzenegger) may be surprised by all the attention given to ceremonious behavior and speech. The poem's plot is indeed driven by the hero's three *agons*, but the actual fighting occupies only a modest fraction of the poem's 3,182 lines. Far more attention is given to direct speech, which make up on average 40 out of 100 lines. In most cases it is not the quick give and take of conversation, but more formal declamations. Part of the reason for so much talking is that unlike *The Wife's Lament*, for example, the narrative perspective does not peer inside the characters' thoughts and emotions.

Famously, the poem begins,

> HWÆT!
> WE GAR-DEna in geardagum
> þeodcyninga þrym gefrunon,
> hu ða æþelingas ellen fremedon.
> (*Beowulf* lines 1–3)

> We have learned of the glory of the Spear-Danes, people's kings, in days of old, how the princes performed noble deeds.

In the virtuoso complexity of the opening syntax and the speculation of what *hwæt* may mean (it is left untranslated here), it is easy to lose track of *we*, the modest subject of the clause, and its verb *gefrunon*, which means "to learn by asking." The pronoun unobtrusively draws each reader into an imagined collective audience that has already somehow "learned" the events that are about to unfold. The moment passes quickly as the narrative proceeds, but it conditions the reader to place the narrative in a larger context of historical lore that (while imagined to be accessible) is distant enough that *we* are not the same as the *they* who populate the world of the poem. At irregular intervals in the poem the first person pronoun reappears in formulaic variants of "I have heard," subtly reminding the reader of this historical distance. For most of the poem, however, the narrative is told (using the conventional terms) from a third person, limited point of view. We may know that Hrothgar, the king of the Danes, feels a deep emotional bond to Beowulf and is saddened at the prospect of his departure from his royal hall Heorot, but the narrative reveals Hrothgar's emotion primarily through his words, his embrace, and his tears. Although the narrative tells us that Hrothgar has secret longing, *dyrne langað*, for Beowulf (line 1879), it does not develop it with techniques of psychological realism that one might find in, say, a Jane Austen novel.

Yet even with its focus on the spoken words and action, the narrative manages to give insight to the thoughts and feelings of the characters. Thus, for instance, when Beowulf contemplates his final battle against the dragon, his thoughts are conveyed through an extensive speech that, in its complex musings, places his immediate decision in a richly layered context that includes the history of antagonism between his tribe the Geats and their enemies the Swedes, an accidental killing in the Geatish royal family with disastrous consequences, and an extended allegory about a father who loses a son in a way that cannot be compensated for (2426–508). It is as if all these separate narratives bring unbearable pressure to bear on his deliberations, and they in some way stand as analogues to internal psychological forces.[11] The technique is so oblique that it resists paraphrase, yet it leads the audience to sense the moral anguish engulfing Beowulf as he weighs the consequences of his decision to fight the dragon.

The poem consistently singles out the ability to wield words as a measure of heroic virtue. When Hrothgar in earlier years has success as a king of the Danes, he decides to build the greatest of halls:

> scop him Heort naman
> se þe his wordes geweald   wide hæfde,
> he beot ne aleh,   beagas dælde
> sinc æt symle.
>
> (78–81)

He who had extensive power of his word shaped for it the name Heorot, he did not belie his vow [*beot*], he distributed rings and treasure at banquet.

Here the *weald* of his word operates on three levels: the command he gives to his followers to build the hall, the naming of Heorot, and the vow to distribute treasure to his followers. It is an altogether exemplary use of language for a king. A hero like Beowulf needs to show a different kind of aptitude with words. When he arrives as a relative stranger to the Danish court he must pass an oral examination. After Unferth publicly challenges Beowulf's credentials as a champion by claiming that Breca defeated him in a test of strength on the high seas, Hrothgar and his court pay attention to the way Beowulf refutes him (499–606). The *how* is at least as important as the *what*. In fact despite Beowulf's rhetorical dismantling of Unferth, which he caps off with a charge of fratricide, neither the modern reader nor the audience in Heorot is in any position to judge the truth claims of one man's account against the other. But Beowulf has the last word, after which the Danes turn with laughter (*hleahtor*) to their feast.

Despite all the talking in *Beowulf*, not many lines in total are given over to vows. Even so, it is clear that everyone, excluding the monsters, holds them solemn. The poet is careful to include a *beot* before each encounter with a monster, but they are given in a variety of formulations. Beowulf's clearest statement of his heroic boast before fighting Grendel comes shortly after his dispute with Unferth, when he tells the Danish queen Wealhtheow of his intention to rid the hall of the monster or die in the effort. "Those words, the *gilpcwide* of the Geat, pleased the woman well" (639–40). His next *gylp-word* (675) comes just as the Geats, now guarding the hall for the Danes, settle down for the night, when he vows not to use weapons because he hears Grendel fights without them. What seems to be a magnanimous gesture turns out to be a stroke of good luck for Beowulf because, unknown to him, a spell has made Grendel impervious to weapons. Hand-to-hand fighting is the only way he can be defeated.

After learning that Grendel's mother has struck in an unanticipated vengeance killing, Beowulf quickly promises Hrothgar (*Ic . . . þe gehate*, line 1392) that he will seek out the monster no matter where it goes. His third occasion for a vow, before his fight against the dragon, has the added poignancy that it will be his last:

Beowulf maðelode,   beotwordum spræc
niehstan siðe: "Ic geneðde fela
guða on geogoðe;   gyt ic wylle
frod folces weard   fæhðe secan,
mærðum fremman,   gif mec se mansceaða
of eorðsele   ut geseceð."

(2510–15)

Beowulf made a speech, spoke *beot-word* for the last time: "I survived many battles in my youth; yet will I, the wise guardian of the people, seek out the hostility, perform glorious deeds, if the wicked ravager attacks me outside the earth-cave."

The placement of *gyt* ("still, yet") in an alliterating syllable, which is unusual for such a word, makes a pointed but understated contrast between Beowulf's survival of his earlier battles and his anticipated death from the dragon. At one point his speech asserts that he is so resolute to begin fighting that he will forgo a formal *gylp* (2528), although everything about the 25 lines including this denial (the rhetorical trope of *praeteritio*) constitutes a boast. His final words addressed to his companions before the fight are "Courageously I will obtain the gold or else battle, perilous deadly evil, will take your lord" (2535–7). It turns out he obtains the gold *and* dies.

After receiving the wound from the dragon and with his life ebbing away, Beowulf gives a brief inventory of his virtues: he ruled his people well for 50 years, he protected them from enemies, he never provoked hostilities, and, he concludes, "I did not swear many oaths unjustly" (2738–9). It is a classic example of what has come to be known as Anglo-Saxon understatement, because it must mean that he *never* swore false oaths, that he was meticulously honest. Although Beowulf's *treowe* is one measure of his exemplary status as a hero, the poem as a whole explores the limits of vows. What happens when they are misdirected? In an early passage the narrative (which is otherwise admiring of the poem's characters) condemns them for making promises (*geheton*) to false gods at their pagan shrines (175–88). What happens when vows are not kept? *Beowulf* gives two striking examples of broken oaths leading to tragic bloodshed. They both take place within the context of a royal marriage arranged to promote peace between two tribes with longstanding enmity. In the "Finnsburh episode" (1068–159) violence erupts between the Frisians and a party of Danes who had been welcomed as visitors presumably to see Hildeburh, the daughter of the Danish king who was given as a "peace-pledge" bride to Finn, the Frisian king. It is unclear why the violence breaks out, although the poem says "Hildeburh had no reason to praise the *treowe* of the Jutes," which implies that they somehow provoked it by violating a pledge. Eventually oaths are sworn between the Danes and the Frisians to conclude the initial outbreak of violence, and the truce survives the long winter when they are obliged to share the Frisians' hall. For the Danes, however, the promptings for vengeance remain so great that when spring arrives their leader Hengest succumbs to pressure to exact revenge and renew the fighting, despite his earlier oath. The Frisians are defeated, Finn is killed, and his hall is looted. The story is told with repeated reference to Hildeburh, because she lost her son, her husband, and a brother after pledges were not honored. In the end the Danes take her with them back to Denmark.

Later in the poem, when Beowulf returns to the Geats after his exploits at Heorot, his account to his king Hygelac takes a curious detour to describe how Hrothgar's daughter Freawaru (who was never mentioned earlier) is destined to be given in marriage to the Heathobards. Perhaps the reader is to understand that Beowulf picked up news of this future marriage during his time in Denmark, but even so his words take on the quality of a prophecy or at least a confident prediction by someone who is now wise enough to see future consequences. The pledge of peace between the Danes and Heathobards, Beowulf predicts, will fail because some members of Freawaru's honor guard will parade around the hall wearing the weapons and armor stripped from Heathobard heroes who were killed in earlier battles against the Danes – the very hostilities that the marriage is designed to end. An old warrior (*eald æsc-wiga*) will goad a youngster to take vengeance, which will doom the chances for peace; "then on both sides the oaths [*að-sweord*] of earls will be broken" (2064). As important as oaths are, especially those designed to curtail violence, Beowulf has learned how precarious they can be, and his assertion that he has always kept his word – his *treowe* – is as much a measure of his heroism as are his physical strength, his courage, and his eagerness for fame.

2

The Hall

The morning after Beowulf has killed Grendel, Hrothgar arrives with Wealhtheow to survey the aftermath of the fighting in Heorot. Someone has already mounted Grendel's arm as a kind of trophy on the outside of the hall. Hrothgar pauses before going in:

> he to healle geong
> stod on stapole,   geseah steapne hrof
> golde fahne   ond Grendles hond
> (*Beowulf* 925–7)

he went to the hall, stood on the *stapol*, saw the gold-decorated steep roof and Grendel's hand.

In its immediate narrative context this passage introduces Hrothgar's speech of praise for Beowulf, but its details foreground the physical presence of the hall as a site loaded with special significance. The precise meaning of *stapol* is not known, but it is almost certainly a structural feature such as a support pillar or a step which Hrothgar mounts on his way up to the door. Whether he stands next to a pillar or on a step, however, Hrothgar's position dramatizes a threshold moment physically, poised as he is between the outside and the inside of the hall, and temporally with Grendel's depredations finished and a happier prospect for the Danes lying ahead. (No one anticipates the attack by Grendel's mother that evening.) In ridding Heorot of Grendel, Beowulf does more than make it safe for sleeping; he restores vigor to the social life of the Danes, because the hall in *Beowulf* functions as a metonym of the society centered in it. A well-ordered hall is a sign of a healthy kingdom. For Hrothgar there was no question of abandoning

Heorot and building a substitute in a safer location (a pragmatic solution in "real life" perhaps, but not in the world of legend). Instead, the retainers who in happier times would sleep in the hall found other quarters in the complex of buildings surrounding Heorot, and each morning everyone returned after Grendel had retreated to the fens. So for 12 years Hrothgar's people could use the hall only during daylight hours. Yet although there was something rotten in the state of Denmark, the narrative suggests that Hrothgar's ability to maintain his kingdom's prominence in spite of Grendel is a measure of his status as a wise king. How many other kingdoms could survive such a pestilence at their core?

Later centuries might heap similar connotations of royal power on other objects such as a crown (think of Prince Henry's meditation on his father's crown in Shakespeare's *Henry IV part II*), but for the Anglo-Saxons it was the hall, which had even broader meanings that extended beyond the individual king to society as a whole. But before we explore its range of figurative meanings, what did an early Germanic royal hall look like? The answer is surprisingly elusive, because in the early Middle Ages most large structures across northern Europe were made of wood, most of which have long since vanished with little trace over the intervening millennium. Recent archaeological work has revealed the basic features of high-status sites in England and elsewhere.[1] The main buildings were large, rectangular, timber-framed structures with steeply sloping roofs and gables on either end. The roof might be thatch or shingle, and the floor was made of wooden planks elevated from the ground. A large fire pit ran down the middle, and holes high in the gables let out the smoke. The building materials made the halls susceptible to fire, whether accidental or set by enemies (the poem alludes to Heorot's future destruction because of the treachery of King Hrothgar's nephew Hrothulf). But wooden construction had its advantages. The building techniques mastered by the Anglo-Saxons enabled them to erect structures with a spacious, open interior, where both the official activities of the court and the mundane activities like eating and sleeping could go on. The halls could be made warm and water-tight. The eighth-century scholar Bede tells a story of conversion in his *Ecclesiastical History of the English People*, which uses the physical features of a hall to great effect. Shortly before the year 600, Bede tells us, Bishop Paulinus traveled from Kent to the court of King Edwin of Northumbria in the hope of converting him to Christianity. The strategy, quite common at the time, was to convert from the "top down," so that after the king was baptized his people would be expected to follow suit. Paulinus presents a compelling case to Edwin, but like a good Anglo-Saxon king he turns to his closest advisors, the *witan*, for their thoughts on the matter. One of them is an anonymous ealdorman (the highest secular rank below the king), who explains his thoughts by means of an extended simile. According to our old religion, he says, life on earth is like the flight of a sparrow through a hall on a winter's night. Inside where the people are banqueting there is fire and warmth, and for the brief interval when the sparrow is in the hall it is warm and comfortable before it flies out again into the storms of winter. Human life is like that fleeting moment in the hall, and our old religion cannot tell us what happens in the bleakness before and after. If Christianity promises something better, concludes the ealdorman, "it is worthy that we should follow it" (*Guide* p. 218, line 37).

As impressive as they may once have been as architectural structures, however, Anglo-Saxon halls suffer in comparison now, because they have long since disappeared, and the stone-built castles that still dot the landscape of Europe reinforce today's romanticized notions of what sites of power in the Middle Ages "should" look like. To our eyes the big wooden halls may resemble nothing so much as barns.

Modern idealizations are not the only kind. No matter how accurate the archaeological reconstructions are, the results need to be applied to imaginative literature like *Beowulf* with caution. It is impossible to know exactly how fanciful the poem's description of Heorot is (was the roof of any real hall adorned with gold?), but it seems a safe assumption that many of the basic features should ring true to the poem's Anglo-Saxon audience, just as the weapons and armor, however archaic, should be imaginable. So when the poem says the hall-wood resounded (*heal-wudu dynede*, 1317), the audience then as now can imagine the noise the planking on a raised floor would make when armored men marched across it. Occasionally, even historically inaccurate details can give a sense of verisimilitude, as when Beowulf and his men approach Heorot on a stone-paved road, which is generally assumed to refer to a Roman road because Germanic people did not pave their roads. Although Roman roads were never built in Denmark, they were nevertheless part of the landscape of medieval

The reconstructed Viking Fyrkat royal hall in Jutland, Denmark.
Photograph by Karsten Kristiansen, 2003.

England, so the poem's Anglo-Saxon audience would presumably accept the detail as realistic.

Whatever its physical features, Heorot projects a symbolic importance that is hard to overstate. Hrothgar's people carve a civilized space out of the wild northern woods and mark it with an architectural monument that is a public measure of young King Hrothgar's success. He commands it to be built and adorned with gold, and given the name Heorot, meaning "hart," an animal thought to have royal significance (67–81). No sooner is its initial description complete ("high and wide-gabled") than the poem foretells Heorot's destruction by fire (81–5), but despite its ultimate fate the hall's physical presence proclaims the Danes' military and political power:

> þæt wæs foremærost   foldbuendum
> receda under roderum   on þæm se rica bad;
> lixte se leoma   ofer landa fela.
>
> (309–11)

It was the greatest hall for humans under the heavens in which the powerful one [Hrothgar] lived; that light shone over many lands.

The light emanating from Heorot, of course, calls to mind both the shimmering brightness of the gold decorating its roof and the outward projection of Hrothgar's political influence. Thus the hall's occupation by Grendel, who inhabits "the treasure-decked hall on dark nights" (*sincfage sel sweartum nihtum*, 167), strikes a blow at the very heart of the Danes' identity.

During the day the Danes carry on as though nothing is wrong. Hrothgar still commands an impressive retinue of veteran retainers (*duguð*) and young warriors (*geogoð*) who have had success on the battlefield and, more important, know how to conduct themselves. When he introduces Beowulf, Wulfgar stands properly before Hrothgar because, the poet tells us, "he knew the old warriors' customs" (*duguðe þeaw*, 359). Wealhtheow, who earlier performs her ceremonial duties of pouring the beer for her husband and others, is explicit about the proper behavior of the men. She tells Beowulf:

> "Her is æghwylc eorl   oþrum getrywe
> modes milde   mandrihtne hold,
> þegnas syndon geþwære,   þeod ealgearo,
> druncne dryhtguman   doð swa ic bidde."
>
> (1228–31)

> "Here each man is loyal to others, gentle in spirit, loyal to their lord, thanes are united, the people fully prepared, warriors after drinking do as I request."

When Beowulf returns home to Hygelac and the Geats, he paints a similarly ideal portrait of the Danish court:

> "Weorod wæs on wynne;   ne seah ic widan feorh
> under heofones hwealf   healsittendra
> medudream maran.   Hwilum mæru cwen
> friðusibb folca   flet eall geondhwearf,
> bædde byre geonge,   oft hio beahwriðan
> secge sealde   ær hie to setle geong."
>
> (2014–19)

"The band was festive; I have never seen greater mead-joys of hall-dwellers under the expanse of heaven. At times the illustrious queen, the pledge of peace, circulated throughout the hall, she exhorted the young boys, often she gave a ring-band to a warrior before she went to her seat."

An important measure of a well-functioning hall is the level of happiness (*dream, sæl, wynn*), helped along by music, poetry, drinking, and hall-entertainment (*heal-gamen*). The drinking lifts the spirits, of course, but it also has a ceremonial function, as Wealhtheow illustrates with the careful distribution of ale down the hierarchy beginning with her husband. When she says *druncne dryhtguman doð swa ic bidde* it does not mean that warriors do what she requests only when they are drunk and no other time. Rather, their ceremonious drinking is just one aspect of their exemplary behavior. However, too much drinking could lead to trouble. Beowulf, for example, suggests that Unferth's aggressive verbal challenge to his credentials as a hero is motivated at least in part by beer: "Well, my friend Unferth, after drinking beer you have said much about Breca" (530–1; see also 1467).

While revelry is a sign of a well-functioning hall, it is the consequence of social cohesiveness at a more basic level, which achieves its most tangible form in the distribution of gifts from a leader to his followers. It seems only appropriate that Hrothgar gives Beowulf magnificent gifts as a reward for defeating Grendel and later his mother. But what may strike the modern reader as odd is that Beowulf turns over his new-found wealth to Hygelac and Hygd, the king and queen of the Geats, immediately upon his return home. Why does he surrender what he jeopardized his life to earn? The quick answer to this question is that our notions of ownership are shaped by deeply ingrained principles of capitalism, which promotes an intimate association between an individual's labor and private property. But the world of *Beowulf* operates within a different economic system, one where gift-giving holds a prominent place. Put simply, a warrior turns over his winnings to his lord, who then adds it to the *hord* for distribution to deserving followers. To adjust Tacitus' formulation, the followers not only fight for the leader, but they obtain booty for him as well. They can, however, keep what the lord doles out, and Hygelac recognizes Beowulf's deeds by presenting him with a splendid sword, which once belonged to the late King Hrethel (Beowulf's grandfather and

Hygelac's father – thus keeping it in the family). Hygelac also gives Beowulf a vast amount of land and his own hall with a *brego-stol*, "the seat of a ruler." In purely economic terms, Beowulf and Hygelac exchange an enormous amount of wealth, but the symbolic meaning is no less weighty. While the text is somewhat vague, Hygelac's gift of a *brego-stol* seems to give Beowulf royal powers, making him an under-king of the Geats (2190–9).

A reciprocal relation attached the receiver of the gift to the giver, a relation that took the form of absolute loyalty, so even if Beowulf is given royal powers he is nevertheless bound as a subordinate to Hrothgar. The clearest statement of this principle comes after Beowulf has died, and the ten retainers who had taken refuge in the woods come forward. The narrative calls them "cowardly traitors," *tydre treow-logan* (2847). The rebuke by Wiglaf, the only retainer who went to help Beowulf, is stinging in the way it turns their splendid armor into badges of shame:

> "He who wishes to speak the truth, alas, can say that the lord who gave out the treasures, the war-gear which you stand in there – when he as prince often gave helmet and armor, the finest he was able to find far or near, to retainers on the ale-bench – that he utterly, completely threw away the war-gear when battle assailed him. The people's king had no reason at all to boast of his comrades in arms." (2864–74)

It may seem that the narrative and Wiglaf are unfairly harsh in their judgments, because Beowulf's last order to his followers was to stay in the woods out of harm's way while he fought the dragon (2529–35). Besides, Beowulf was the only one with a metal shield that could offer protection from the dragon's flames. But Wiglaf's point is that loyalty should override any individual command especially when the king's life is in danger, and Wiglaf points to their armor as a tangible and obvious sign of their obligations (2850).

If loyalty is the supreme virtue of a retainer, then generosity becomes the paramount virtue of a king, and the site for distributing wealth is so closely associated with the hall that the act of gift-giving becomes a way of identifying the structure itself. Some epithets for a hall include *gold-sele*, "gold-hall," *hring-sele*, "ring-hall," and *gif-heall*, where the king's throne may be called a *gif-stol*, "gift-seat." There is a similar constellation of terms for king, *gold-gyfa*, *gold-wine*, "gold-friend," etc. A good king will distribute enough treasure to command the loyalty of his troops, who will in turn acquire more when they are successful in battle. The armor and jewelry they wear become visible signs of their social status, because the superior retainers are rewarded with the best equipment after they have proven their worth. When Beowulf and his companions first arrive in Geatland the coastguard who confronts them is struck by Beowulf's impressive appearance: "I have never seen a greater warrior across the earth than a particular one among you: that is no *seldguma* honored with weapons" (247–50). There is some uncertainty about exactly what *seld-guma* means in this passage. Literally it means "hall-man," but does it have derogatory connotations similar to today's "armchair general" or "couch potato"? Or does the passage mean "he is not a follower but rather a *leader* of men"? In either case it is both Beowulf's physical size and his impressive armor that announce to the coastguard that here is someone special. These attributes along with his exceptional speaking ability are his public credentials as someone of high standing, even before he has a chance to display his fighting ability.

The hall, however, is not always presented as a well-adjusted social entity in *Beowulf*, which provides a range of examples from the ideal to the dysfunctional. Some passages dramatize the terrible violence that can erupt, as with Beowulf's prediction of the violent failure of Freawaru's planned marriage to the Heathobards (2020–69, discussed in the last chapter). The Finn episode (1063–159) also foregrounds the hall as an important site for uncontrollable violence, as chapter 1 points out. But the *Beowulf* passage is not the only account of the *Fres-wæl* or "Frisian slaughter." A single manuscript leaf containing a fragment from another Old English poem concerning the same event survived long enough for a transcript to be printed in 1705 (after which the leaf was lost). Later editors have identified it by a number of names, including "The Finnesburg Fragment" (Wrenn pp. 213–15), "The Battle of Finnesburh" (*Beowulf* pp. 212–15), and "The Fight at Finnsburg" (Klaeber pp. 231–8). The 48 lines that comprise the fragment are enough to show it is clearly an episode from a longer poem. The surviving lines limit the point of view to what the Danes can see from inside their hall, presumably a guest-hall large enough to hold 60 men, and it seems to narrate the initial outbreak of violence, when Jutes in the service of the Frisian king attack the Danes in a night raid. It celebrates the heroic behavior of the fighters more than the corresponding episode in *Beowulf*, which circles back to the grief of Hildeburh and the lamentable failure of the peace pledges to hold. The fragment also hints that the crucial points of attack in a hall are, not surprisingly, the doors, which the Danes successfully defend for five days. The obvious expedient of setting fire to the hall to force out the defenders was considered less heroic, if not downright cowardly, if parallels from *Njal's Saga* and other Icelandic sagas are any indication.[2]

Other examples from *Beowulf* point to the failure of the hall as a unifying institution when, for example, one of Hrothgar's thanes eulogizes Beowulf in verse by making a favorable comparison with Sigemund. He follows it with a digression on Heremod, who as an earlier successful Danish king eventually changed for the worse and came to a bad end (867–915). Hrothgar again brings up Heremod as a negative exemplum in his long admonition to Beowulf after he defeats Grendel's mother. "You will become a lasting help and comfort to your people," he says, unlike Heremod, who became vicious, bloody-minded, and "never gave rings to the Danes in pursuit of glory," *nallas beagas geaf / Denum æfter dome* (1707–20). The moral of Hrothgar's lesson is not hard to fathom: a good king is generous to his followers.

The extended episode of the dragon is dominated by an antithetical model of the hall, because "the powerful enemy of the people guarded a certain treasure-hall [*hord-ærn*] in the earth for three hundred years" (2278–80). The dragon is not merely a fascinating if dangerous force of nature. It is evil because it hoards treasure in a cave, a point the narrative reinforces by repeatedly and ironically referring to its cave as a "hall" (*dryht-sele, eorð-reced, hring-sele, reced*), where in human society the treasure would be put into useful circulation. The dragon also retaliates for the theft of an object from its treasure-hoard by destroying Beowulf's royal hall:

> bolda selest   brynewylmum mealt
> gifstol Geata.
>
> (2326–7)

the best of halls, the gift-throne of the Geats, melted in the surging flames.

Its destruction brings Beowulf "the greatest heart-sorrows," *hyge-sorga mæst* (2328), and moves him to fight the dragon even though it means certain death.

The recurring wars between the royal families of the Swedes and Geats create an ominous backdrop to much of the action in the last third of the poem, as has often been pointed out. But adding to the sense of foreboding are references to the imperiling or destroying of halls, such as the dragon's destruction of the Geats' royal hall. The dragon acquires his hoard only after some unknown tribe perishes, but before the last survivor dies, he places the treasure in a hidden cave and utters (as the narrative imagines) a poignant lament addressed to the earth:

> "Heald þu nu, hruse, nu hæleð ne mostan
> eorla æhte. Hwæt, hyt ær on ðe
> gode begeaton; guðdeað fornam
> feorhbealo frecne fyra gehwylcne
> leoda minra þara ðe þis lif ofgeaf:
> gesawon seledream."
>
> (2247–52)

"Earth, hold the possessions of warriors now that men can no longer do so. Virtuous ones once obtained it from you; death in battle, perilous deadly evil took each of the men of my people who gave up this life: they saw hall-joys."

The treasure becomes a metonym of the hall, which becomes a metonym of the happiness that the survivor's society once enjoyed, and the greatest sorrow derives from its dissolution, signaled here by consigning the precious metal back to the earth from which it was once mined. The "they" who saw hall-joys are most likely the men who are lamented, but the entire address begins with the treasures (*æhte*), which have also "seen" the hall-joys that they helped create. The survivor goes on to catalogue the joys that have passed:

> "Næs hearpan wyn
> gomen gleobeames ne god hafoc
> geond sæl swingeð ne se swifta mearh
> burhstede beateð."
>
> (2262–5)

"There is no pleasure of the harp, joy of the lyre, nor does a good hawk fly through the hall, nor does a swift horse stomp in the courtyard."

Even though the dragon merely found the cave with the unattended treasure and took possession of it (as dragons instinctively do, 2270–7), it is in some way complicit with the human tragedy that led to the hoard's abandonment – or at least it keeps the treasure from the good things it can do when it is in human society. The centerpiece of Beowulf's long meditation before fighting the dragon is another imaginative invocation of a desolate hall, or more precisely the desolation of a man whose son is killed on the gallows. He can expect no recompense for the death and, as Beowulf describes it, his grief finds what T. S. Eliot calls an objective correlative in his son's empty hall:

> "gesyhð sorhcearig   on his suna bure
> winsele westne   windge reste
> reote berofene.   Ridend swefað
> hæleð in hoðman;   nis þær hearpan sweg
> gomen in geardum   swylce ðær iu wæron."
>
> (2455–9)

"Sorrowing he looks upon his son's chamber, the desolate wine-hall, the windy resting place deprived of joys. Horsemen, warriors sleep in the grave; no sound of the harp, no joy in the yard is there where they once were."

While the dragon presents one kind of antithetical hall, Grendel's mother presents another. Her water-bound cave is consistently described as a hall, but the parodic inversion comes not from hoarding treasure but from the way she welcomes her guest, Beowulf, and the description of her cave as a hall. "Then the earl perceived that he was in some unknown hostile hall [nið-sele] where no water might harm him in any way nor could the sudden grasp of the flood touch him because of the roofed hall [hrof-sele]" (1512–16). The scenes from Hrothgar's court that surround the fight with Grendel's mother remind the audience (if reminding is needed) of the proper decorum in a hall: how a stranger is greeted, queried, and shown hospitality. Wealhtheow, moreover, gives a positive example of the woman's ceremonious function. In the Grendelkin's hall Beowulf is called a guest (gist, 1522, and sele-gyst, 1545) but instead of hospitality he encounters an aggressive "mighty water-woman" (mere-wif mihtig, 1519) who attacks to kill. Of course Beowulf is an attacker and not a guest, and her cave is not a hall (flet, reced), but the repeated use of such terms is an unsubtle way of calling attention to the norms of human behavior in this monstrous perversion of a well-ordered hall-society, which Beowulf can eliminate only by becoming as monstrous as his adversaries.

Immediately following *Beowulf* in its manuscript is *Judith*, a fragment containing the final 349 lines of a poem that was once longer by perhaps as much as 1,000 lines. It is an imaginative recasting of the Latin Vulgate Book of Judith, which throughout the Middle Ages was generally considered a canonical book of the Bible but in more recent centuries has had a more marginal status.[3] The Latin tells the story of a beautiful and brave widow named Judith, whose Samaritan town Bethulia is besieged by an invading Assyrian army led by a formidable champion named Holofernes. Judith volunteers to visit the enemy camp with an ambiguous plan that involves using her beauty to seduce Holofernes. When she first presents herself to him, he is struck by her beauty, and on the fourth day sends for her to join him at a feast. When she arrives "the heart of Holofernes was smitten, for he was burning with the desire of her" (12:16), but by the time the feasting ends, he has drunk himself into unconsciousness. Left alone with him in his chamber and using his own sword Judith decapitates Holofernes, then puts his severed head into a bag and quietly leaves the Assyrian camp for Bethulia. The Israelites, seizing the opportunity, rout the Assyrians, who are terror-stricken once they realize their leader is dead.

We are fortunate that the surviving portion from the Old English poem contains the concluding episodes from the original story, beginning just before Holofernes's feast, but it is also long enough to give a clear idea of the extent to which the Old English poem modifies the Latin prose. It simplifies the plot so that only Judith and Holofernes are identified by name, and the other characters recede into the background, which has the effect of making the conflict more starkly a battle between good and evil.

Even more remarkable, however, are the changes in adopting traditional motifs for character and setting. Although their feasting takes place in a tent, Holofernes's men become hall-retainers (*flet-sittende, benc-sittende*) who wear coats of mail and other Germanic armor. Holofernes is a gold-friend of men (*gold-wine gumena*), but these heroic terms drip with irony because the Assyrians are the anti-types of traditional heroes from legends like that of Beowulf. They show no decorous speech or behavior. Holofernes, for example, roars and clamors and urges his men on in a bout of binge-drinking: "So the wicked, stern-minded dispenser of treasure [*sinces brytta*] induced his warriors to drink [*drencte*] wine all day until they lay in a swoon, he inebriated [*ofer-drencte*] all his men as if they were mortally slain, drained of every virtue" (*Guide* 28–32). At the end of the carousing he calls for his new concubine, Judith, so that he can "violate the beautiful woman with defilement and sin" (58–9). The extant Old English lines do not call her a widow, although that detail may be lost from the part of the poem that has not survived. Instead the most common terms for her are *ides* and *mægð*, the former carrying connotations of nobility (usually "lady") and the latter of youth (often "maiden").

Similarly the Old English version preserves the specific virtues attributed by the Latin source to Judith, but the terms draw from the Germanic poetic tradition. She is wise (*gleaw, snotor*), brave (*ellen-rof*), and, most remarkably, *ælf-scinu*, a word that literally means something like "elf-shimmering" but has connotations of preternatural and even deceptive beauty. After drawing Holofernes's sword she prays to God for help, then pulls Holofernes's head shamefully (*bysmerlice*, 100) until it is stretched out. The decapitation takes two blows, a grisly detail retained from the Latin which suggests that despite her other virtues Judith is not physically strong. By the same token the feat she performs to save her people is not a miracle but a marvel. It has more in common with the exploits of a folk hero like Beowulf than a miracle performed through a saint, where God's power intervenes in the natural world to do something that is otherwise impossible.

After Judith returns to Bethulia she speaks to the citizens and urges them in conventional Germanic language to battle. Her exhortation greatly expands the more restrained Latin and ends: "Your enemies are condemned to death and you will have glory, honor in the battle, as the mighty Lord has signaled to you through my hand" (195–8). The ensuing battle scene is drawn out with obvious relish, and it includes the traditional "beasts of battle" motif (205–11) and some comic relief as the timid Assyrian officers hesitate to disturb their chief, who they assume is luxuriating in bed after a night of sex and excessive drinking. The description of the rout ends with most of the Assyrians meeting their death. The defeated invaders leave behind so much booty that it takes the warriors of Bethulia a month to collect it all, and they give to Judith as her portion all of the wealth once owned by Holofernes. Does this gesture, taken over from the biblical narrative but translated into a Germanic context, suggest that the warriors acknowledge her as a military leader? In any case Judith is a complex character, combining traits of hostage, concubine, warrior, saint, and a leader of her people.

Exodus is even more ambitious in recasting a biblical story in the ethos of Germanic heroic poetry. It begins with a traditional epic flourish that foregrounds Moses's role as history's great lawgiver, a role that King Alfred also singled out for Moses at the beginning of his code of Anglo-Saxon law in the late ninth century:

> *Hwæt!* we have learned far and near across the earth of Moses speaking the laws, the extraordinary lawcode for generations of men, for every blessed one in heaven as a reward for life after the baleful journey, a lasting counsel for warriors, for every living person. Let everyone hear it who will! (*Anthology* lines 1–7)

The laws (*domas*) span all of human history since Moses. They have served previous generations of humans up to the present day, and even the saints in the afterlife celebrate Moses's lawcode (*word-riht*) for bringing them to enjoy the rewards of heavenly bliss. But the poem quickly shifts focus to Moses's role as a wise general who leads his people out of Egypt. There is no doubt about his virtues as a leader:

> He wæs leof Gode, leoda aldor,
> horsc ond hreðergleaw, herges wisa,
> freom folctoga.
>
> (12–14)

> He was beloved by God, the commander of tribes, quick-minded and wise, the army's leader, the brave prince of the people.

The language of *Exodus* is remarkable for its poetic complexity, which combines imaginative figures of speech with a tightly controlled meter. It shows a remarkable ability to fuse the traditional epic language into the biblical story, where the desert sands become indistinguishable from the desolate heaths (*mor*) of northern Europe. As the Israelite *fyrd* ("army") begins its journey, one notable line exactly repeats a description of the forbidding countryside leading to the underwater home of Grendel's mother, where the party of Danes and Geats travel across *enge anpaðas, uncuð gelad* ("narrow single-file paths, an unknown way," *Exodus* 58, *Beowulf* 1410). A particularly brilliant passage begins with an arresting instance of synaesthesia just before the waters come crashing over Pharoah's army, "the sky above grew dark with the voices of the doomed" (462–3). As the plot reaches its climactic action the poem exploits the ability of the half-lines to switch rapidly from one perspective to another to capture mimetically the chaos and confusion as the Egyptian army is caught up in the flood, where the scenes shift like quick cinematic cuts among close-ups of the warriors, the water pouring in, the seabed, the sky, and epithets for God (464–97). By the end, the Egyptians become a "flood-pale army" (*flod-blac here*, 498).

The title of the poem is somewhat misleading, because it retells only a small part of the Latin Vulgate Book of Exodus, but the exodus of the people of Israel from the land of Egypt became, in Christian exegesis, a central *figura* of their faith. Psalm 113, which had been used in the last offices for the dying and for the burial of the dead, begins "When Israel went out of Egypt, the house of Jacob from a barbarous people, Judea was made his sanctuary, Israel his dominion."[4] In a later century Dante's "Letter to Can Grande" famously uses this passage to give a quick illustration of the fourfold operation of Christian exegesis, paraphrased here: at the literal level it means the exodus of the Children of Israel from Egypt at the time of Moses; as an allegory it means the individual Christian's redemption brought about by Christ; on the moral level it means the conversion of the soul from sin to a state of grace; on the anagogical level it means the departure of the soul from the slavery of earthly corruption to the eternal rewards of heaven.[5] Dante was merely using the psalm to illustrate the various levels of the figural or allegorical reading of scriptures, but he chose the exodus of the Children of Israel as a clear and uncontroversial example. There is no indication that the Old English poet had all four meanings in mind, but Dante is still pertinent for showing the pervasive way that episodes from the Old Testament were interpreted as a *figura* of their fulfillment in the New Testament, and further how they could be applied to other levels of Christian history. The Old English poem's translation of the episode into terms familiar to its audience merely extends the figural interpretation in another direction, where the historical event of long ago can apply to the life of individual Christians in Anglo-Saxon England.

Exodus does not offer extended examples of the Germanic hall, in large part because the events take place when the people are away from a settled home. But in summarizing their victory, Moses observes, "Lacking a homeland we occupy this guest-hall" (534–5), where the *gyst-sele* means the transitory world. He then speaks of the Last Judgment, where the Lord will meet every soul "in that meeting-place" (*on þam meðel-stede*, 543) and welcome the blessed *duguð* into heaven. Clearly Moses is directing the poem's Anglo-Saxon audience toward an anagogical interpretation of the events, using the language of heroic poetry. Moses goes on to say (554–64) that God has fulfilled the promise (*gehet*) he once made to their forefathers with the swearing of oaths (*mid að-sware*) that if they kept the holy teaching they would overcome their enemies and enjoy a victorious kingdom (*sige-rice*), the beer-halls of warriors (*beor-selas beorna*). Heaven never looked quite so much like Valhalla.

Another heaven appointed as a Germanic hall is constructed within a 2,936-line poem called *Genesis*, which expansively narrates from the first 22 chapters of the Old Testament. A section of over 500 lines stands out from the rest because of its language and versification. It is commonly called *Genesis B* (or *The Saxon Genesis*) and recounts the story of Satan's banishment from heaven, followed by the temptation of Adam and Eve. Unlike the rest of *Genesis* and indeed most biblical poems, *Genesis B* is a reworking not from the Latin Vulgate but from a poem in Old Saxon (the language once spoken in what is today western Germany). This separate translation was then at some point inserted into the longer narrative that uses the Latin Book of Genesis as its source. The Bible, many people are surprised to learn, has never contained a full narrative of the fall of the angels. It has always been an apocryphal story, yet one with such wide currency in Christendom that it was usually accepted as if it were canonical. Its origins are early. Because angels and devils are not mentioned in either of the Genesis accounts of creation, early Jewish commentators created a narrative to account for their presence in other passages from scripture, such as one from Isaiah, which gives the basic outlines of the now-familiar story: "How art thou fallen from heaven, O Lucifer, who didst rise in the morning? . . . And thou saidst in thy heart: I will ascend into heaven, I will exalt my throne above the stars of God, I will sit in the mountain of the covenant, in the sides of the north . . . But yet thou shalt be brought down to hell, into the depth of the pit" (Isaiah 14:12–15).

The Old Saxon and Old English writers brought a wealth of traditional formulas and themes to the plot elements of a prince's rebellion, the high throne, and the subsequent banishment. Among all the ten orders of angels created by God, the story begins, he showed special favor to one whom he made more beautiful than the rest. But this angel began to be excessively proud (*ofer-mod*) and began to utter hateful speech (*hete-spræce*) and vaunting words (*gylp-word*) against God on his high throne. The ironic understatement carried by the narrative's use of verbs of seeming and thinking is delicious even in paraphrase: this angel could not find in his heart that he wished to be in God's service; it seemed to him that he had more strength and skill than God; it seemed that on his own he could make a throne higher in the heavens; he doubted that he would become God's vassal. The audience already knows that the rebellious angel (yet to be named Satan) will get his comeuppance, but he seals his fate with a defiant speech, beginning "Why must I toil (*winnan*)? . . . there is no need for me to have a lord" (*Reader* p. 129, lines 278–9). He has enough power to make a more splendid throne (*godlecran stol*) higher in heaven. There is nothing qualified or nuanced about his rebellion: *Ic mæg wesan god swa he* (283). Because Anglo-Saxon scribes did not capitalize the name of the deity (a later convention), the passage just given could be translated one of two ways, both equally damning: "I can be God just as he is," *or* "I can be a god just as he is." (It could even mean "I can be as *good* as he is.") The rebel boasts of strong companions who will remain loyal to him, and thus he concludes, "I will no longer be his subordinate" (291).

God of course hears it all, becomes angry (*gebolgen*, 299), and throws him from the high throne – with apparent ease. The rebel angel began his defiant speech by asking *Hwæt sceal ic winnan?* The narrative answers his rhetorical question, "He had obtained [*gewunnen*] hatred from his Lord; he had lost his mercy" (301). He and his companions are banished to a hell with fire that gives suffocating smoke and no light, and its heat is broken only by a freezing wind from the east. Remarkably, he is still a king and still defiant, and now in a puny act of creation shapes (*sceop*) for himself the name Satan (345). His kingdom, though, is a constrained place (*ænga styde*, 356) because he is bound by chains. As bad as the physical torment is, he is even more anguished by the thought that Adam is destined to possess the high throne he made in heaven (364–7). He then plots how he can turn Adam and Eve from God and enlists one of his followers to tempt them. Satan cannot do it himself, because he will lie bound forever, the powerless king of a diabolical hall. Fire may consume an earthly building like Heorot, but it is the very stuff that Satan's hall consists of.

The imaginative projection of Germanic hall-life onto the foreign landscapes of *Judith, Exodus,* and *Genesis B* is a deliberate anachronism calculated to drive home the moral lessons of the biblical stories to their medieval audience. It is not a failure of imagination, as though the Anglo-Saxons were incapable of conceiving other buildings or other models of communal life. The Bible itself provided them with many alternatives, and more locally across the landscape of England they encountered the remnants of Roman buildings made from brick and stone. The poem now known as *The Ruin* is a meditation based on what are apparently the remains of a Roman bath such as those at Bath itself. But in an uncanny instance of form mimicking content, *The Ruin* has itself been eaten away by old age (*ældo under-eotone*) (*Guide* 6), thanks to a hole burnt through the last 14 folios of the Exeter Book, which holds the only copy of the poem. Even though about one quarter of the poem's original 49 lines have been damaged, enough remains to give a fairly good idea of its overall form. It begins with a description of the physical ruins, which it admiringly calls "the work of giants," *enta geweorc* (2). The awe expressed in the very first word, *wrætlic,* "wondrous," is divided between the impressiveness of the physical structures and the forces that damage them. Even though they long outlasted the master-builders (*waldend-wyrhtan,* 7), the buildings are undermined by the passing of time, by natural forces, and by fate itself. Meditation on the impressive remains leads to imaginative speculation of what life was like in their heyday. Here the poem turns to the traditional hall-themes of Old English literature: the sound of warriors, a mead hall full of human joys (*mon-dreama,* 23), "until powerful fate reversed that" (*oþþæt þæt onwende wyrd seo swiþe,* 24). Death in various forms overtakes the inhabitants. They are not merely warriors, builders, and mead-drinkers, but repairers (*betend,* 28), a role that adds a new dimension to the theme of transience, because their activity implies that humans *can* keep the ravages of time in check, but only by constant labor. As splendid as these past builders and inhabitants were, *wlonc ond win-gal* ("proud and flushed with wine," 34), their accomplishment could endure only by a precarious balance between forces of destruction and the ceaseless human efforts to maintain civilization, here represented by the physical buildings. The poem ends with tantalizing fragments about the workings of the hot baths, which it notes were "convenient" (*hyðelic*, 41). *The Ruin* is not quite an example of the age-old theme of *ubi sunt qui ante nos fuerunt* ("Where are those who went before us"), because there is no mystery about the fate of past inhabitants: they have fallen just like the buildings (*crungon*, 25, 28, 31). And although the poem speaks admiringly, it does not convey any hope, wistful or otherwise, for their return. It does, however, use the ruins for a meditation on transience, which overtakes every human culture no matter how splendid.

Another poem in which ruined buildings prompt a similar meditation is *The Wanderer*, where the narrative voice observes that it is a mark of wisdom to perceive how all the wealth of this world stands desolate, just as the walls of buildings stand exposed to the elements (73–7). It continues,

> Woriað þa winsalo,   waldend licgað
> dreame bidrorene,   duguþ eal gecrong,
> wlonc bi wealle.
>
> *(Guide 78–80)*

The wine-halls decay, the rulers lie deprived of joy, all the proud troop perished by the wall.

The verbal similarities with *The Ruin* are striking (*waldend, dream, gecrong, wlonc, weal*), and even extend to the description of the walls as *enta geweorc* (87, *Ruin* 2), but it is unlikely that one poem borrowed from the other, because the movement from observing the remnants of the past to a contemplation of the transience of this world most likely draws from traditional themes and formulas. Moreover, the lines quoted from *The Wanderer* come from the middle of a 115-line poem that has a more complex structure than *The Ruin*.

The thematic similarities, however, are not limited to these two poems. They extend to a group of poems that Old English scholars have long called elegy, which in classical Latin and Greek is a well-established genre – a lyric poem on a serious topic using a particular metrical form. The genre was later imitated and introduced into English by the scholar-poets of the Renaissance, who narrowed its topic to a lamentation for the dead and set aside the earlier association with meter. This later genre (not the classical) lies behind the practice of calling the Old English poems elegies, which seem to constitute an analogous but independent Germanic tradition of meditative lyrics concerning loss and sometimes consolation. If they are not strictly lamentations for the dead, they often incorporate the death of loved ones as part of the larger theme. Most strikingly, both the older and newer traditions in English adopt a personal perspective to explore the psychological experience of grief, from which they may turn to a transcendental level to find consolation. "Tradition" certainly applies to the well-attested and self-conscious classical and humanist genres, but it is perhaps too confident a word for the Old English elegies commonly cited, which are scattered throughout the second half of the Exeter Book. They include many of those discussed in these first two chapters: *Wulf and Eadwacer, The Wife's Lament, The Husband's Message, The Ruin, Deor, The Wanderer,* and *The Seafarer.*

The last two on this list, *The Wanderer* and *The Seafarer,* are among the best-known poems in the Old English corpus. They are paired together in almost every anthology and critical survey – and with good reason. They are found within a few folios of each other in the Exeter Book and are of a similar length. Both are extended monologues that subordinate plot to lyric introspection. While both are elegies, they also have affinities with another generic grouping called wisdom literature, illustrated in aphoristic lines like "Whoever maintains his good faith is praiseworthy" (*Wanderer* 112) and "Whoever does not fear his Lord is foolish" (*Seafarer, Guide* 106). Both concern solitary travelers whose journey away from the centers of civilization becomes a master-metaphor for the trials of life. Both incorporate the themes of exile, transience, loss, memory, separation, solitude, fate, death, harsh weather, anxiety, noble behavior, and past civilizations. Both have particularly enigmatic passages that have provoked a variety of interpretations. Modern readers, including Ezra Pound and W. H. Auden, have found their lyrical movement from physical desolation to psychological introspection especially congenial. They are also the most Christian of all the elegies, confidently placing their hope for consolation in the eternal rewards of heaven and forsaking the transitory pleasures of earth.

Yet they are nevertheless quite different from one another. Almost all of *The Wanderer* is a first-person monologue by *eard-stapa* (literally, "earth-stepper," 6), who gives the poem its name. He begins by lamenting his *ceare* (9), which he utters every morning, and which exploits the heroic motifs centered on life in the hall. He is *sele-dreorig* (literally, "hall-sad," 25), and he can find happiness only in a *meodu-heal* with a *sinces brytta* (25–7). He remembers happier times with hall-thanes and treasure-receiving (*sele-secgas ond sinc-þege*, 34), but that has all perished. When sorrow and fatigue bind him in sleep, he dreams:

> þinceð him on mode   þæt he his mondryhten
> clyppe and cysse   ond on cneo lecge
> honda ond heafod,   swa he hwilum ær
> in geardagum   giefstolas breac.
>
> (41–4)

It seems to him in his mind that he embraces and kisses his lord, and lays hands and head on his knee, just as he had enjoyed the gift-throne for a while in earlier days.

The gestures between the Wanderer and his lord seem to have the formal quality of ritual, but they are also highly personal and affectionate. It sometimes surprises the modern reader to find so many emotive terms used to describe the relationship between a lord and a retainer. Loyalty is one thing, but we are conditioned to be suspicious of affective attachments where there is (as we say) an asymmetry of power. But an Anglo-Saxon lord is nothing if not beloved (*leof*) and a friend (*wine, freond, gold-wine, wine-dryhten*). These terms are about as common as any other epithets for a lord, such as those concerning his generosity or power. It was not only accepted but noble behavior to give such a public display of same-sex affection in the Middle Ages, contrary to the formal aloofness or phobia in modern Western societies, especially among men.[6]

When the dreamer awakes he sees seabirds, falling hail, and snow, which trigger yet more sorrow as he recalls past companions, who like the birds *swimmað oft onweg* ("often swim away," 53). Not only do the birds become objective correlatives of his desolation, but there is an almost hallucinatory blending of birds and memory in lines 50–7, where the "companions of men" and "the spirit of the floating ones" could be taken – at least fleetingly – as the seabirds as well as the memory of friends. (Most editions differ in how they punctuate and interpret these lines.) In any case, the speaker often sends his weary spirit over the frozen waves (57) where it travels with the seabirds.

After contemplating the physical ruins of the *eald enta geweorc* (87, discussed above), the poem begins to generate a moral, beginning with an especially poignant *ubi sunt* passage:

> "Hwær cwom mearg? Hwær cwom mago?   Hwær cwom
>   maþþumgyfa?
> Hwær cwom symbla gesetu?   Hwær sindon seledreamas?
> Eala beorht bune!   Eala byrnwiga!
> Eala þeodnes þrym!   Hu seo þrag gewat,
> genap under nihthelm,   swa heo no wære."
>
> (92–6)

"Where is the mare? Where is the kinsman? Where is the treasure-giver? Where are the seats of the feast? Where are the hall-joys? Alas, bright goblet! Alas, mailed warrior! Alas, glory of the people! How the time has departed, has grown dark under the cover of night, as if it had never been."

The poem's answer to the rhetorical questions are the final words spoken by the *eard-stapa*, who finds that all the glories of the earth are fleeting or *læne* (which literally means "on loan"): "Here money is transitory [*læne*], here a friend is transitory, here human life is transitory, here kin is transitory, the foundation of this earth will become completely empty!" (108–10). The poem ends with several lines of timeless gnomic wisdom that circle back to the first line of the poem to find *ar*, meaning "mercy, grace, honor," and locates the only permanent consolation in *Fæder in heofonum* (115) where all stability stands.

The Seafarer likewise concludes by placing its hope in *seo ar of heofonum* ("the mercy of heaven," line 107), but its path to that realization takes a different route. The difference can be measured in the two poems' attitudes toward fate. The Wanderer finds himself a victim of the impersonal forces of *wyrd* (*Wanderer* 15), where the Seafarer sees *wyrd* as synonymous with God's power (*Seafarer* 115), to which he voluntarily submits himself. Where the Wanderer resigns himself to the mutability of the world that leaves him an exile, the first person narrator of *The Seafarer* actively if inscrutably seeks out the paths of an exile (*wræccan lastum*, 15) by turning to the sea and all the perils it presents. The first 33 lines describe in careful detail the physical and emotional suffering of life on the sea. While his feet are bound with frost in the exposed prow of the ship, sorrows sigh hotly around the heart (8–11). Deprived of human companions, he finds the cries of seabirds are a comfortless substitute for the sounds of revelry (19–26). While the prosperous people in cities, *wlonc ond wingal* (29), have no idea of the hardships he endures (27–30, 55–7), his heart always prompts him to sea to travel to the land of foreigners (38).

In a passage reminiscent of *The Wanderer's* seabirds blending into memories, the speaker's *hyge* ("memory/thoughts/emotions"[7]) ranges far over the sea and returns,

> gifre ond grædig,   gielleð anfloga
> hweteð on hwælweg   hreþer unwearnum
> ofer holma gelagu.   Forþon me hatran sind
> Dryhtnes dreamas   þonne þis deade lif,
> læne on londe.   Ic gelyfe no
> þæt him eorðwelan   ece stondað.
>
> (62–7)

ravenous and greedy, the solitary flyer cries out, it urges the heart irresistibly over the expanse of water. Therefore the joys of the Lord are more ardent for me than this mortal, transitory life on land. In no way do I believe that the earth's riches stand forever.

The passage moves from a physical description of the solitary bird returning from its flight over the water, which becomes the objective correlative of his *hyge* that urges the seafarer's heart to another voyage. The causal linking of *forþon*, "therefore," is a crucial if inexplicable turn of syntax – it employs a term of logic for an urge that is irrational – but one of the essential lessons learned by the Seafarer is that the joys of heaven cannot be comprehended by earthly standards, which are *deade* and *læne* even in their most splendid manifestation.

The Seafarer is more sparing in its invocation of the life of the hall than *The Wanderer*, in large part because the first person narrator *voluntarily* exiles himself from human civilization. The first mention of a ship, *ceol* (5), is immediately followed by a synonym, *cear-seld*, which literally means "sorrow-hall." The collocation of the two words sets up a contrast that operates throughout the poem, especially in those passages that itemize the pleasures denied to the Seafarer, such as *song, gomen, medo-drinc, hearp, hring-þege* (the receiving of rings) (20–2, 44). The earthly delights given up by the Seafarer are precisely those associated with a hall.

Almost no first-hand information about the activities in a hall have come down to us: there is nothing as detailed as a "program" of entertainments. We know poems were delivered in oral performance, but what kind and how often? Were they spoken or sung? If sung, was there always a harp accompanying? What other kinds of musical instruments were there? Other kinds of singing? Was there an order to ceremonies? How was the drink served? How much of a problem was drunkenness? Violence? Were there rituals for distributing treasure and how often was it done? What was the physical condition of a typical hall for light, warmth, weatherproofing, and cleanliness? What were the furnishings? We know halls were decorated with tapestries, but to what extent? And what were the tapestries and other decorations like? Were the inside walls painted? Was it a noisy place? How crowded was it?

Works of imaginative literature in Old English can give tantalizing glimpses, but their halls are almost certainly idealized. And the glimpses from poems like *Beowulf* and *The Wanderer* tell us more about the poetic performances than any other aspect of hall life, not only because their narratives refer to them, but also because they are specimens of what might have formed part of the *heal-gomen*. But such impressions from the literature need to be approached with caution, because the poems that survive today were transcribed by literate clerics, not orally trained *scopas* ("oral poets") like those imagined in *Beowulf*, so the surviving corpus was subjected to an unofficial clerical censorship that skewed the selections away from what secular audiences actually heard. On the other hand we should not insist on an emphatic division either between what the clergy and the lay found entertaining or between the literate and the oral.

Sometimes evidence for hall-entertainments comes from unlikely sources. Shortly before 800 CE an English-born abbot named Alcuin (one of the most accomplished scholars associated with the court of Charlemagne) sent a Latin letter offering pastoral advice to a Mercian bishop known only by his pen name "Speratus." Among other things Alcuin urges him to preach well, read often, give alms, and perform the liturgies with proper reverence. A lengthy paragraph warns against the sin of gluttony and includes a pointed excursus on drunkenness. But another passage condemns the practice of listening to a "harpist" and "pagan song" at the bishop's table. Most editions of *Beowulf* print this excerpt from Alcuin's letter as evidence that the otherwise shadowy character named Ingeld was familiar to Anglo-Saxon audiences from now-lost sources, because in his letter Alcuin famously asks "What has Ingeld to do with Christ?"[8] The answer of course is "Nothing," and Bishop Speratus should chase such heroes and their storytellers from his table. From our historical distance we cannot tell if Speratus actually listened to harps and poems of pagan heroes like Ingeld or if Alcuin was indulging in a generalization, but his letter strongly suggests that such legends were part of the fare in secular halls. It also suggests that it was possible for bishops to retain some of the trappings of hall-life in their households around the year 800. Whether it was still possible in the decades around the year 1000, during the Benedictine reform and when most surviving Old English poems were copied, is more doubtful, but Alcuin's letter can still remind us that the wall separating the clergy from the laity was permeable. The clergy were born into the secular world, after all, and presumably they did not always abjure their taste for vernacular literature when they took their vows.

The short lyric *Deor*, usually counted among the elegies, is enigmatic in many of its details, but its subject matter clearly belongs with Ingeld in the hall. It is one of the few Old English poems consisting of stanzas, each of which alludes to a legendary character who met with adversity: Weland the famous smith had his hamstrings cut by his patron King Nithhad; Nithhad's daughter Beaduhild was later raped by Weland and became pregnant by him; almost nothing is known about the "sorrowful love" (*Eight* line 16) of Mæthhild and Geat; Theodoric was exiled for 30 years from the Huns; the fifth and final stanza begins in general terms about one who is troubled by sorrow before it identifies the speaker of the poem, Deor, who had favor in his lord's court until a *leoþ-cræftig* ("song-skilled," 40) rival took his place. By leaving his stanza until the end, Deor (whether a fictional name or not) signals that his grief is as great as any suffered for the other disasters. The allusions also display the virtuoso reach of his repertory as a *scop*. Each stanza ends with a refrain, *Þæs ofereode; þisses swa mæg*, "That passed away; so can this." *Þæs* refers in a general way to the misfortune that each stanza alludes to, but the referent for

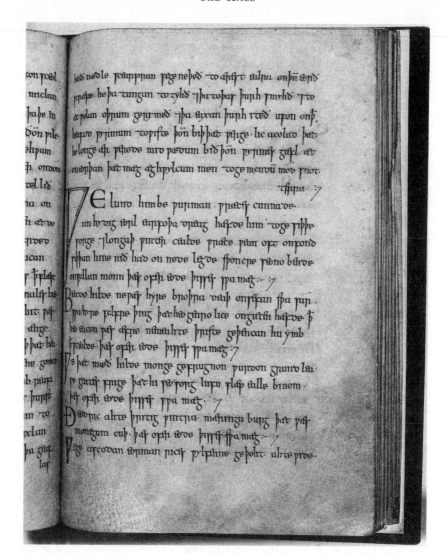

The beginning of *Deor* in the Exeter Book. Notice the triangular shape of
the letter *wynn,* and the use of capitals to mark off stanzaic divisions.
Exeter Cathedral 3501, folio 100a, reproduced by permission of the Dean
and Chapter of Exeter Cathedral Library.

þisses is ambiguous until the final stanza, when the voice of Deor locates "this" within his present desolation. It is not a hopeful or consolatory conclusion for Deor, because the crucial word in the stanza is the auxiliary *mæg*, which means that hard times *can* pass, not that they will.

A poem even more allusive than *Deor* and just as congenial to the world of the hall takes its name from the speaker identified in the very first word, *Widsið maðolade, wordhord onleac,* "Widsith spoke, unlocked his word-hoard" (*Beowulf* p. 196). The name literally means "wide traveler," and he surveys in 143 lines of verse all the luminaries he has ever known and visited (which some quick calculations show to be an impossible task geographically and chronologically). It seems to be a poet's poem, because much of it reads like a loosely ordered inventory of heroic characters, strung together in alliterating lines, who might populate a narrative poem. The raw material, for example, could end up in poems like those concerning the deadly fight between Hnæf and Finn, or the story of Ingeld the Heathobard, or a hall named Heorot built by Hrothgar – each of whom is mentioned in *Widsith*.

When King Edwin was deliberating whether to convert to Christianity, one of his ealdormen invoked the metaphor of the hall to illustrate his thinking on the matter (as discussed at the beginning of this chapter). The conversion in Northumbria and elsewhere in England inaugurated a large-scale transformation that introduced not just a new religion, but eventually a tradition of Latin scholarship, a technology of writing, and other aspects of Mediterranean culture, the full effects of which Edwin could scarcely imagine. Two generations later (around 670), his grand-niece Hild officiated over another occasion of cultural change that also had profound repercussions, but this one took place far from the glamor of the royal hall. It involved a farmhand who forged a new synthesis of paganism and Christianity, and of oral and written poetry. It begins at a feast where peasants were improvising their own hall-entertainment on a scale far humbler than in the rarefied world of *Beowulf*. What happened was a small miracle, as the next chapter shows.

3

The Miracle

The best-known story from Bede's *Ecclesiastical History of the English People* (731) concerns a peasant named Cædmon who miraculously received the gift of poetry. He was one of the laborers attached to a monastery in Northumbria, called Streoneshealh in Bede's time, later Whitby, and his job was to tend the cattle. Whenever the laborers had a feast, Bede tells us, it was their custom to pass around a harp and take turns entertaining one another with song. But Cædmon would have none of it. Whenever the harp approached, he would excuse himself from the feast (*gebeor-scip*) out of shame (*for scome*), a reaction that suggests how unusual it was for anyone to refuse the harp. Performing poetry was the social norm. On one such evening Cædmon took refuge in a cattle-shed to visit the livestock under his care, where he fell asleep. Someone appeared to him in a dream, called him by name, and asked him, *Cedmon, sing me hwæthwugu*, "Cædmon, sing something for me" (*Guide* p. 222, line 28). Cædmon protested he did not know how to sing, but the stranger persisted until Cædmon asked *Hwæt sceal ic singan?* He said, *Sing me frum-sceaft* ("Sing creation") (32–3). Immediately Cædmon improvised a short song in praise of God the creator. The next morning when word of his new gift reached Hild, the monastery's abbess, she gathered a group of Whitby's most accomplished scholars and teachers to test whether it was of divine origin. They told Cædmon holy stories and asked him to turn them into verse. He went back to his home overnight and returned the next day to give back the stories in song "adorned with the best poetry" (59–60). Convinced that Cædmon had indeed received a gift from God, Abbess Hild urged him to take monastic vows and join the community, where he continued to learn stories from salvation history and created songs on topics from creation to the Last Judgment. (None of these other poems is known to survive.) He led an exemplary life as a brother, Bede's chapter concludes, and died a saintly death.

The poem now known as *Cædmon's Hymn* may seem unremarkable at first glance. Within its nine lines it has eight epithets for God, and it follows a rather simple thematic progression from beginning to end. The following version is written in a northern dialect of Old English from the eighth century, similar to what Hild and Cædmon actually spoke. It is transcribed from a manuscript now in St Petersburg, Russia, and preserves the original spelling and punctuation:

> Nu scilun herga   hefenricæs uard
> metudæs mehti   and his modgithanc
> uerc uuldurfadur   sue he uundra gihuæs
> eci dryctin   or astelidæ
> he ærist scop   ældu barnum
> hefen to hrofæ   halig sceppend
> tha middingard   moncynnæs uard
> eci dryctin   æfter tiadæ
> firum foldu   frea allmehtig.
>   (adapted from *Anthology* p. 2)

> We now have to praise the heavenly kingdom's guardian,
> the might of the creator and his purpose,
> the work of the glory-father as he
> the eternal lord established the beginning of every wonder.
> First he, the holy creator, shaped heaven as a roof
> for the children of generations.
> Then the guardian of mankind, the eternal lord
> afterwards adorned the middle-earth,
> the land for humans, the almighty lord.

The Old English epithets for God are underlined, and they show at a glance that little space is left for anything except a brief prayer of praise followed by the miracle of creation in two stages: first the sky, then the land. In the St Petersburg manuscript the words are written out in three long lines across the bottom of the folio below the Latin account of *Cædmon's Hymn* in Bede's *History*. What is printed here puts the words into verse lines, but it preserves the Northumbrian spelling and the solitary mark of punctuation at the end. It also retains the only capital letter, the first word "Nu." Note in particular that none of the epithets for God was capitalized. The lack of capitalization was not a sign of disrespect – in fact scribes did not capitalize any names at this time. Modern editions of Old English poems customarily supply capitals and marks of punctuation where present-day conventions call for them, but here the older conventions are preserved to give an idea of the medieval experience of reading poems in manuscript.

Even with the full complement of modern editing signals, however, the early Northumbrian dialect would still look unusual. Elsewhere in this book the Old English texts come from later centuries and are printed in the West Saxon dialect, which even to inexperienced eyes looks quite different from Cædmon's language. What makes the difference seem even greater, however, is the absence of the letters eth <ð> and thorn <þ>, and the use of <u> as a consonant. At this early date scribes were still experimenting with the best way to transcribe their native tongue. Eventually they supplemented the Latin alphabet with eth, thorn, and another letter from the runic alphabet called wynn <ƿ> for the sound of [w].

Despite the poem's utter simplicity, the Anglo-Saxons must have recognized something special about *Cædmon's Hymn* because 22 manuscript copies (an unusually large number) survived into the modern period, most of which were added, like this one, to Latin versions of Bede's *History*. To these early readers the episode represented something more than a quaint story of an adult man suddenly acquiring the gift of poetry, which was a rather modest miracle in comparison with most others in Bede's *Ecclesiastical History*. Cædmon's epithets for God, such as *hefen-ricæs uard, uuldur-fadur,* and *eci dryctin,* are crucial in understanding his innovations. They were created by using the older formulas as a template on or in which a new term was added or substituted. Where a pagan god may be *mehtig,* Cædmon's God is *all-mehtig;* where a mortal king is *dryctin* ("lord") or *ricæs uard* ("guardian of the kingdom"), God becomes *eci dryctin* and *hefen-ricæs uard.* Although the changes are technically simple their consequences are far-reaching. In making the traditional verse a suitable vehicle for Christian themes, Cædmon legitimized it for every Anglo-Saxon including the clerical elite. Bede recognized the profound consequences of Cædmon's new gift, which did more than turn a cowherd into a local celebrity. When he followed the stranger's instructions to sing *frum-sceaft*, "creation" became more than the theme: Cædmon literally sang into existence a new species of poetry.

For centuries before Cædmon the Anglo-Saxons and other Germanic people had cultivated an oral verse form with an intricate meter and a specialized poetic vocabulary that made extensive use of formulas. It was sophisticated in its conventions but far different from the Latin and Hebrew traditions that shaped the literature emanating from the Roman church. The precise way that Bede narrates Cædmon's dream may subtly promote the oral tradition, because for a *visio* it has surprisingly few visual details. The figure who stands by him is described in both the Latin (*quidam*) and Old English (*sum mon*) as merely "someone" (not an angel as is sometimes said), who seems to be a disembodied voice. There is no physical description. The entire dream takes place on the level of spoken language, first as dialogue and then as the poem, as if orality itself were the crucial subtext. In the later exchange between Hild's Latin scholars and the illiterate poet, Bede dramatizes two further innovations: the oral tradition's ability to shift from its old legends to literature for source material, and the capacity of Old English to translate a language as venerated as Latin. This multiple validation of the vernacular (in religion, literary source material, and its status next to Latin) may seem unremarkable today, but in the seventh century it was revolutionary – or to use a term more congenial to the time, it was miraculous. One of the things miracles do in Bede's *History* (and elsewhere) is to signal God's approval. After Cædmon sang to Whitby's finest, the cultural distance between the *scop* and the scribe had to dwindle. As the introduction to this book points out, when Hild welcomed Cædmon into the monastery, Old English poetry gained access to the scriptorium, which created the possibility of vernacular literature.

Bede does not mention whether Cædmon's other songs were committed to writing, and there is little doubt that Whitby had the means to make copies like the one in the St Petersburg manuscript, but as a monastery its energies were directed elsewhere. Like some other early foundations in England, it was a double monastery with separate houses for monks and nuns, and under its first abbess, Hild (657–80), it became, using Bede's metaphor, a brilliant jewel that illuminated all of Britain.[1] The story of Cædmon follows a chapter of the *Ecclesiastical*

History on the life of Hild, who was known for her prudence and whose monastery produced five bishops for England. Because Whitby was a short distance from Bede's monastery in Jarrow and because his lifetime (*c.*673–735) overlapped with that of Hild (d. 685) and perhaps even that of Brother Cædmon himself, Bede very likely derived at least some of his information from first-hand sources. Thanks to the *Ecclesiastical History* Cædmon is the earliest English poet known by name and one of the best-documented. The next named poet is Bede himself, who on his deathbed composed an intricate five-line poem in his native tongue, according to one of his students, who preserved it: "In the face of the final journey no one becomes wiser than is needed to think before his departure how his soul will be judged as good or evil after his death-day."

Among its other accomplishments, Whitby produced one of the two earliest saints' lives in England, a Latin life of Pope Gregory I (d. 604), who was especially revered among the Anglo-Saxons because of his instrumental role in evangelizing them. The other early life celebrates the enormously influential Northumbrian saint, Cuthbert, and was written within two decades after his death in 687. A generation later Bede continued this local interest in Gregory and Cuthbert. He devoted lengthy sections of his *Ecclesiastical History* to each and promoted Cuthbert's growing cult with a prose "life and miracles of St Cuthbert, bishop of Lindisfarne," *after* he had composed a metrical life in 979 Latin hexameters. Hagiography was a pervasive and well-developed medieval genre with roots in the early church. Its purpose was to provide an inspiring model for Christians to follow and to promote a saint's cult by demonstrating divine signs of his or her holiness. Hagiographies were not biographies in the modern sense. The genre evolved various conventional features, which included (among others) early signs of divine favor, an ascetic lifestyle, struggles against temptation, and a saintly death, but however much the particulars of one life differed from the next, at each crucial stage the saint's holiness is proven by miracles. And the miracles continue after death, usually in connection with the physical remains: hair, bones, clothing, and so on. It was not merely a literary trope. The abiding physical presence of the saint in his or her relics and their potential for miracles were such an essential part of a cult that religious foundations went to great – and sometimes scandalous – lengths to secure them.[2]

Old English saints' lives are commonly based on Latin sources, but they often show significant modifications, because the vernacular expanded the potential audience from the educated clergy to just about any Anglo-Saxon. Hence they often have a more didactic tone. Guthlac (d. 714) was an Anglo-Saxon saint, roughly contemporary to Bede, whose Latin *Life* by Felix was commissioned by Ælfwald, king of the East Anglians, some time between 720 and 749. Guthlac was born into a noble Mercian family and served for nine years as a soldier before entering religious life, finally becoming a hermit in the fens near Crowland. The Latin *Life* was translated more than once into Old English, and two poems on Guthlac by different authors appear consecutively in the Exeter Book, together making up 1,378 lines.[3] *Guthlac A* (which seems to draw from sources independent of Felix) offers a discursive and dramatic account of his struggles as a hermit before he is rescued by a miraculous visit from St Bartholomew, and *Guthlac B* narrates Guthlac's exemplary but painful death. Although he turned from life as a soldier to a *halig cempa*, "holy soldier," neither poem indulges in the full potential of the poetic conventions of the saint-as-hero.

By contrast, other poems such as *Juliana* and *Andreas* exploit many conventions of the heroic tradition, which they elaborately announce in their opening flourishes.[4] In their plots they are fairly conventional saints' lives drawn from Latin sources. Juliana is a virgin-martyr who against her father's wishes refuses to marry a wealthy heathen. She is whipped and imprisoned for her obstinacy. In the dramatic centerpiece of the poem she is tempted by the devil (called *wær-loga*, "pledge breaker," among other things), whom she commandingly resists and then compels to confess his evil deeds. Finally she is executed, but not before she exhorts the onlookers to turn to God. *Andreas* begins with the imprisonment and torture of Matthew by the depraved Mermedonians, who threaten to eat him. God sends Andrew (that is, Andreas) to rescue him, which he does after a risky sea voyage, imprisonment, restoring Matthew's sight, and a miraculous escape. Finally Andrew triumphantly converts his persecutors.

Immediately following *Andreas* in the Vercelli Book is *The Fates of the Apostles*, which some have seen as a continuation of the story of Andrew and Matthew. It also begins with language that echoes *Beowulf*'s opening, but curiously the epic "I" is anxious and not the self-confident conveyor of a collective tradition:

Hwæt! ic þysne sang   siðgeomor fand
on seocum sefan,   samnode wide,
hu þa æðelingas   ellen cyðdon,
torhte ond tireadige.   Twelfe wæron,
dædum domfæste,   Dryhtne gecorene,
leofe on life.   Lof wide sprang,
miht ond mærðo,   ofer middangeard,
Þeodnes þegna –   þrym unlytel.
(adapted from *Anthology* 1–8)

Weary from life, I found this song in my troubled heart, assembled it
from far and wide, how the bright and glorious princes revealed their
courage. The twelve were famous in deed, chosen by the Lord, beloved
in their life. The praise, power, glory and boundless majesty of the Lord's
thanes extended far and wide across the earth.

For the next 80 lines or so the poem gives short summaries of the
saintly careers and martyrdom of each apostle, following the order
Peter, Paul, Andrew, John, James, Phillip, Bartholomew, Thomas,
Matthew, James, Simon, and Thaddeus. (Matthias is missing from the
list, but Paul rounds up the number to twelve.) Few biographical
details are given, but heroic epithets abound: Bartholomew is *beadu-
cræftig beorn* ("battle-skilled warrior," 44), James is *stiþ-mod* ("stout-
hearted," 72), and so on. When each apostle is martyred he dies bravely,
even eagerly, like a conventional Germanic thane defending his lord.
Thomas is *collen-ferð* ("bold-hearted," 54), and he is also the only one
who performs a miracle, bringing a king's brother back to life (54–7).
Nevertheless, a *sweord-ræs* ("sword-onrush," 59) takes Thomas's life
and his soul seeks out its heavenly reward.

Beginning with line 88 the poem shifts direction and mentions
once again the narrator's anxious state of mind. By bravely and
willingly accepting martyrdom the apostles gained salvation, but
the narrator implies he is an ordinary sinner who must appeal for
help from friends when he has to go on the lonely journey of death.
There follows a short passage (98–105) with disjointed, gnomic-
sounding sentiments, but within the half-lines are runic letters. Runes
were an alphabet used by Germanic people before their conversion,
when Christianity brought its well-developed technology of writing
using the Latin alphabet (which you are seeing on display here). The
use of runes continued for special purposes after conversion, and they

often carried over from their older uses connotations of secrecy and magic. It was customary to name each runic character after a word beginning with the letter's sound; thus *feoh*, for example, is the name for the rune <ᚠ>. In the passage from *The Fates* the word identifying each rune has a role to play in the syntax and meter of the line, but taken consecutively as letters they spell FWULCYN – from which, the narrator predicts, anyone "wise in forethought" (*fore-þances gleaw*, 96) can perceive who composed *þas fitte* ("this song," 98). Shifted around the letters spell "Cynwulf," or more conventionally "Cynewulf."

    The Fates of the Apostles is one of four poems with the runic letters for Cynewulf's name woven into lines near the end. During a time when poems were copied and transmitted without attribution (Cædmon's being an exception), it was a bold and ingenious move to adjoin a name in such a way that it could not be changed without affecting the alliteration, meter, and sense of the lines. On the other hand what the runes signified had to be transparent enough for the reader to decipher the name and the pious message containing it. Elsewhere in the Vercelli Book is another "signed" poem, *Elene*, which relates how St Helena (mother of the Roman emperor Constantine) headed an expedition to Jerusalem to find the true cross. It is not strictly speaking a saint's life although it resembles one in the way miracles are used, for example, to reveal the location of the cross and show God's favor toward Elene and her mission. The runic signature in *Elene*, unlike that in *The Fates*, spells out the name in proper order – CYNEWULF – even at the expense of semantics, because three of the runic names strain the meaning of their clauses, but in this case syntax might have been sacrificed for the sake of making the name explicit. The signature is introduced by the narrator's musing on the meaning of the cross as he found it in books. Following the runes are 50 lines of ominous descriptions of the Last Judgment. In *Elene* Cynewulf does not specifically petition the reader for prayers as in *The Fates*, but his signature is surrounded by passages that speak of salvation and divine judgment (*Reader* pp. 177–80).

    The other two poems with Cynewulf's signature, both in the Exeter Book, are *Juliana*, a saint's life discussed above, and a poem on the Ascension known as *Christ II*, which forms the middle of a poetic triptych (hence the names *Christ I, II,* and *III*). As a composite of several poems *Christ* constitutes a total of 1,664 lines at the beginning

The runic letters incorporated into the text of *Juliana* spelling out the name CYNEWULF. Exeter Cathedral 3501, folio 76a. Reproduced by permission of the Dean and Chapter of Exeter Cathedral Library.

of the Exeter Book, and it organizes itself around defining moments of Christ's life – or more specifically around the events that take place *outside* of his human life: before his birth (*Christ I*), after his death (*Christ II*), and at the Last Judgment (*Christ III*). It is not a plot-driven narrative, but a thematically linked series of devotional, hortatory, and didactic passages.

Christ II displays a broad consistency in style with the other poems bearing Cynewulf's runic signature. All four are orthodox in matters of faith, based on Latin sources, yet they show an inventive use of native poetic tradition which can be seen, for example, in *Elene*'s battle scene between Constantine and the invading Huns, in which the emblem of the cross miraculously assures victory. They also show a tendency to sharpen the lines of conflict between good and evil. Although Cynewulf is conversant with the oral style of poetry, the poems are still bookish in their dependence on Latin sources. Even *The Fates of the Apostles*, which has no known source, gestures to what "we have learned through holy books" (*þurg halige bec*, 63). It is common, as in the discussion above, to speak of Cynewulf as if his identity were fixed, but what exactly does the runic signature signify? Does it assert authorship of each poem? Given what we know about the formulaic and anonymous process of composing Old English verse, how confidently can we assume that someone named Cynewulf was the sole author of each poem bearing his name? It is a viable working assumption to think of him like a modern author, but even with the most confident attribution we know precious little about the poet behind the name. The familiarity with Latin sources points to a cleric with some education, and some dialectal features point to Mercia. The question of date is more open but it is unlikely he was as early as Bede.

The attribution of authorship is less problematic in Old English prose, where writers are more likely to affix their names and incorporate biographical information. The most prolific prose writer, and unsurpassed as a stylist, was Ælfric, who began his career as a monk at Cerne Abbas and ended it as the abbot of the Benedictine Abbey at Eynsham (*c*.1010). Ælfric's *Lives of Saints* (*c*.998) is a product of his mature years, when he had mastered his distinctive alliterative prose style. The purpose of the collection, as he describes it in his Old English preface, is to gather the passions and lives of the saints whom monks honor in their services (*Anthology* p. 130, lines 6–7), and the lives are arranged in manuscript according to the order of their feast days on the calendar. Ælfric's collections of homilies (discussed in the next chapter) included saints celebrated more generally throughout the English church, but the *Lives* was more limited in scope. Ælfric selected most of them from a single collection of 165 Latin *vitae* known as the "Cotton-Corpus legendary," originally compiled in northern France or Flanders. But as is characteristic of Ælfric, his translation "in the ordinary English language" adapts his source in the direction of brevity and clarity. As he puts it in the Latin preface:

> We have not been able in this translation always to translate word for word but, rather, we have taken care to translate diligently according to the sense, as we find it in Holy Scripture, in such simple and clear phrases as will profit our listeners. It should also be known that we have abbreviated the longer passions, . . . and brevity does not always disfigure a narrative but many times it makes it more appropriate [*honestiorem*].[5]

Above all, Ælfric's adaptation is motivated by an attempt to make the Christian devotions to these saints comprehensible to a lay audience. The majority of the lives concern martyrs from the early years of the church. It should be noted that Ælfric uses the Latin *passio* ("passion") to refer to the lives of martyrs like Edmund, while *vita* is more often associated with other saints such as virgins and confessors. Among Ælfric's saints are five with local interest – Alban from Roman Britain and another four, Æthelthryth, Swithhun, Oswald, and Edmund, from Anglo-Saxon England – whose *vitae* are not found in his chief source, the Cotton-Corpus legendary. Those that he took from the legendary, on the other hand, were saints like Sebastian, Agatha, and Lucy, generally well known throughout western Christendom.

A short prologue to Ælfric's life of St Edmund gives a fascinating history of an eyewitness account, passed on orally from the time of Edmund's martyrdom (869) up to Dunstan (*c*.909–88). Ælfric first knew Dunstan as one of his early teachers, but Dunstan was better known for his public activities as an abbot, a guiding force behind the Benedictine monastic reforms, and an advisor to kings. Under King Edgar he eventually became archbishop of Canterbury (960), the top ecclesiastical position in England. According to Ælfric, as a young man Edmund's sword-bearer witnessed his lord's death in 869, and as an old man he told the story to King Athelstan (924–39), whose court Dunstan had joined in the years before he was ordained (935). About 50 years later Dunstan related the story to Abbo, a Benedictine monk from the French monastery of Fleury, who visited England for two years (985–7) to advise Dunstan on the monastic reforms. On his return to France Abbo wrote a Latin *Passio Sancti Eadmundi* (dedicated to Dunstan), which then circulated back to England for Ælfric to retranslate (*c.*998). Given the local currency of the story and especially in light of Ælfric's early association with Dunstan, it is likely he also drew from oral accounts.

The story itself is fairly conventional. It begins with an account of Edmund's personal virtues: he was wise, honorable, humble, morally upright, and generous to the poor. One year marauding armies of Danes attacked England, led by two leaders, one of whom named Hinguar stalked and killed the innocent people of East Anglia like a wolf (*swa swa wulf, Guide* p. 198, line 156). Hinguar sends Edmund an ultimatum to give him tribute and submit to him as an under-king, but he responds that he would rather die for his own country than submit to a heathen commander (*hæþenum heretogan*, p. 199, line 194) unless he first accepts the faith of Christ. Edmund apparently lacks an army to defend him, because Hinguar soon enters the royal hall, where Edmund throws down his weapons. The Vikings capture him, beat him with staffs and whips, and for sport they shoot him with spears until he resembles a hedgehog (p. 200, line 214). Finally, they behead him, which is witnessed by *sum man* (Edmund's sword-bearer) who later tells it all "just as we say here" (*swa swa we hit secgað her*, 220–2). As a final act of desecration the Vikings hide the head in dense briars, so Edmund's people cannot find it when they come to claim his body. But God miraculously sends a wolf to protect Edmund's head, which shouts out when the people draw near, *Her! Her! Her!* (238). They find it resting between the front paws of the wolf, which though ravenously hungry has refrained from harming it. (The verbal echo of the earlier simile for Hinguar, *swa swa wulf*, suggests that God has the power to convert even the most savage pagan.) As the people return to town, the wolf follows them up to the outskirts as if it were tame before returning to the woods. After peace returns to East Anglia many years later the people erect a church in honor of the king, but when they open the tomb to move the body, they discover that it is incorrupt, and the neck and head are reattached with only a faint mark to show

how he was slain (p. 201, lines 255–60). Various miracles are witnessed at the tomb, and the soil that soaked his blood when he was beheaded also proves to have miraculous powers. Edmund thus joins the pantheon of English saints (p. 203, lines 318–21).

Why is Ælfric's prose special? He set out to fashion a style that was simple (in comparison with the demanding Latin prose that he was familiar with), but in his hands it evolved into a prose that borrowed rhythmic phrasing and alliterating patterns from Old English poetry. In fact Anglo-Saxon scribes often marked the end of each alliterating line with a raised point, as shown in the following excerpt from *The Life of St Edmund*, which describes how the Vikings hide his head in the briars and how the local people later find it (adapted from *Guide* p. 200, lines 223–8):

> Hwæt ða se flothere   ferde eft to scipe ·
> and behyddon þæt heafod   þæs halgan Eadmundes ·
> on þam þiccum bremelum   þæt hit bebyrged ne wurde ·
> Þa æfter fyrste syððan   hi afarene wæron ·
> com þæt landfolc to   þe þær to lafe was þa ·
> þær heora hlafordes lic   læg butan heafde ·
> and wurdon swiðe sarige   for his slege on mode ·
> and huru þæt hi næfdon   þæt heafod to þam bodige ·

The Viking army went back to their ships and hid the head of the holy Edmund in the thick briars so that it would not be buried. Then after they had been gone for a period of time the inhabitants came to the place where his remains were, where their lord's body lay without a head, and they became distressed in their heart because of his slaying and especially because they did not have the head to the body.

With a little effort even an inexperienced eye can pick out the alliterating sounds, for example, *behyddon, heafod, halgan* in the second line, or the "cross-alliteration" in the sixth: *hlafordes lic læg heafde*. Following the conventions of poetry, alliteration is avoided in the last stressed syllable of the line, but Ælfric did not adopt the specialized poetic vocabulary, the strict meter, and some other conventions from verse. The result flows along in steady increments line by line, but within each are variable rhythms and aural effects. It was a medium that perfectly suited Ælfric's narrative purposes.

The detailed accounts of miracles, which take up about half of the *Life of Edmund*, are not incidental even if they strike most modern readers as tedious. They are essential to the purpose of the saint's life, which was the most typical and prevalent literary genre throughout the Christian Middle Ages. In the Old English preface to *Lives of Saints*, Ælfric claims that miracles are the justification of the book:

> We write many miracles (*wundra*) in this book,
> because God is marvellous (*wundorlic*) in his saints,
> . . . and the miracles (*wundra*) of his saints honor him,
> because he made the miracles (*wundra*) through them.
>   (*Ælfric* p. 121, lines 18–21)

In this formulation (lineated here as verse to reflect the rhythms and wordplay of Ælfric's prose) God's omnipotence is the origin of the miracles, but their ultimate purpose is to honor him – or to use Aristotelian terms, God is both the efficient cause and the final cause. This theocentric circularity, in which God is on the giving and receiving end, was part of the pious appeal of miracles and made their significance all the more potent. In a similar cycle of cause and effect, the saints through their holiness become the means by which God displays his saving power, and the miracles prove the godliness of the saints. For miracles to have any human significance at all, however, they needed to be proclaimed publicly. To do otherwise was to hide their light under a bushel; thus the *vitae* are full of moments of discovery, where God's signs are disclosed to the saint's contemporaries. And the circulation of written saints' lives ensures an even broader dissemination of examples of how Christian faith is validated through their miracles.

While the martyrdom and miracles of St Edmund must have appealed to the medieval audience because of the spectacular and gruesome details, other saints had a more low-key approach to sanctity. For example, Æthelthryth was revered as a saint from the time of the early Anglo-Saxon church, and Ælfric derived the details of her life from Bede's *Ecclesiastical History* (book IV, chapter 9). Like her contemporary Hild, she was the daughter of a king (King Anna of East Anglia), and in her mature years she became the abbess of a monastery that she founded on the isle of Ely in East Anglia. Æthelthryth's specific claim to sanctity was virginity, which she maintained despite being twice married. Her virginity is proven, Ælfric asserts in the first sentence of her life, by the miracles that she frequently performs (*þe heo wyrcð gelome*, Introduction p. 168), where the present tense of the verb makes clear that her miracles continue after her death. During her lifetime, in fact, she performed no *wundor* aside from preserving her virginity.

Two politically advantageous marriages were arranged for Æthelthryth, but in each she persisted *on clænnysse*. The first, to a prominent nobleman, ended with his death after only a few years, and she was next given to Ecgfrith, the king of Northumbria. (We know from other sources he was very young at the time.) Their marriage lasted for 12 years, but despite Ecgfrith's efforts she maintained her virginity and finally convinced him to release her to take vows as a nun. A year later she became abbess at Ely, where she led an exemplary life, fasting, praying for long hours, and bathing only seldom. After eight years a painful tumor grew on her neck, which she gratefully accepted as a suitable penance for the vanity of expensive necklaces in her younger years. Finally a physician was called. He lanced the tumor, and worms crawled out of it (p. 169, sentence 15). At this point, some readers of saints' lives might expect a miraculous cure, but Æthelthryth was a historical Anglo-Saxon saint, and neither Bede nor Ælfric was inclined to embellish his sources. Three days later, after she seemed to be recovering, she died.

Her sanctity was confirmed only after her body was "translated" or reinterred in the church 16 years after her death, when it was found to be incorrupt, and even the tumor on her neck had healed. So her body, which was unblemished by sexual intercourse during her life, was miraculously kept incorrupt after her death. Miracles followed her body's translation. Her old burial clothes, for example, and the water that was used to clean her body were found to have healing powers. Ælfric closes the story with exhortations for married couples to live in purity for the glory of God.

Æthelthryth's living deeds lack the sensational quality of those of many other saints, especially martyrs. Virginity can be defined as a passive virtue, a withholding of activity, which in the case of saints like Æthelthryth provides an unpromising basis for a narrative plot. As with other saints, however, her living deeds are only a prelude to the more valuable proofs of sanctity after death, when miracles at the site of her physical remains can change the faith of spectators at the shrine and readers of her *vita*. Her ability to affect our lives survives to this day, though in a way that is linguistic rather than miraculous. The name "Æthelthryth," despite its opaqueness to English-speakers today, lives on in the curious etymology of the word "tawdry," as any good etymological dictionary will show.

Oswald was another royal English saint whose *passio* Ælfric includes in his *Lives of Saints*, which like the story of Æthelflæd was drawn primarily from Bede's *Ecclesiastical History* (book III). One of the earliest kings during the conversion of Northumbria, Oswald ascended the throne only after his uncle and two successors were killed in the space of two years by the pagan British king Cadwealla. But before he could rule his kingdom Oswald had to defeat Cadwealla. On the morning of the battle he erects a cross and leads his troops in prayer, so God grants him victory over Cadwealla's superior forces because of his faith. After the battle the cross is found to have miraculous powers, and later a church is built over the spot. More than with other saints, Ælfric gives an extended account of the career of Oswald, who after assuming the throne invites the Irish-born monk Aidan from the monastery of Iona to become bishop and to assist him in converting the Northumbrians. The plan succeeds largely because of Aidan's saintly habits. Oswald is also successful in the more conventional aspects of kingship by expanding his kingdom. On a more personal level he is charitable, humble, and virtuous. One Easter during a banquet, Oswald learns that some poor people are waiting outside for alms, and he immediately orders that the food be given to them and even the silver platters cut up for distribution. After Aidan witnesses the king's generosity, he seizes the king's arm and says, "May this blessed right hand never become decayed" (*Reader* p. 80, lines 80–1). After ruling for nine years Oswald is killed in battle by Penda, the pagan king of Mercia, who mutilates the body by decapitation and cutting off his arm. The arm, as Aidan prophesied, is enshrined after it proves to be incorrupt – and Ælfric's use of the present tense *lið* implies that it remains so to his day, "and it lies as sound as it was when it was struck off" (140–1). Oswald's tomb becomes a site for miracles, as does the earth that absorbed his blood when he was killed.

Ælfric ends the life of Oswald by observing that it is no wonder that the king cures the ill "now that he lives in heaven" (216–17), because he helped so many while he was alive. Ælfric for a second time invokes the authority of Bede as his source, an invocation of a kindred spirit because both monks, although separated by almost 300 years, had an abiding interest in perpetuating orthodoxy and an aversion to the more fantastic excesses of some saints' lives.

Even apart from the extensive Latin tradition of saints' lives, Ælfric was not working in a vacuum, although he is the only named author of the genre in Old English. Over 30 anonymous prose lives survive, most from before the year 1000, including those of such stalwarts as Christopher, Guthlac, Margaret, Mary of Egypt, and the Seven Sleepers. But there were also more unusual saints, such as the cross-dressing St Euphrosyne, who in order to become a monk dresses as a man and lives out her life in a monastery. Anglo-Saxon England also had an extensive devotion to Mary that is partly reflected in the Old English apocryphal gospels about her translated from Latin.[6] Excluded from this discussion are the numerous lives incorporated into homilies by Ælfric and others, which offered another means for the laity to learn about saints.

While miracles are an essential ingredient of saints' lives, they are also found in many other aspects of Christian teaching, beginning with holy scripture. Another poem from the Vercelli Book, *The Dream of the Rood*, is a dream vision of extraordinary imaginative power, although the conventional name for it is somewhat unfortunate because it implies that the cross itself has a dream. It begins rather with a first person narrator who announces in the first half-line that he had "the best of dreams," in which he saw the cross elevated in the sky and elaborately adorned with gold and jewels. All creation gazes upon the cross, which is the Lord's messenger (*engel, Guide* line 9), but the initial wordless vision of it reminds him of his sinful state. His sight gains the ability to penetrate "through the gold" (18) to see the suffering once endured by and on the cross, especially the wetness from the flow of blood. The vision vacillates between the splendidly ornamented cross and the more gruesome wooden implement of human torture. The two correspond to iconographically conventional ways of representing the crucifix in Christian art: on one hand the triumphant Christ in an upright, commanding posture, and on the other the suffering Christ with bloody wounds on a sagging, lifeless body. What is innovative in this part of the dreamer's vision, however, is that it is not Christ who triumphs or suffers (yet) but the wooden cross itself.

Beginning in line 28 description gives way to speech as the cross begins to narrate its unique story. It was cut down from a forest and made into an instrument for public executions. The clause, *heton me heora wergas hebban* (31) has a double meaning shown in the two possible translations: "they ordered their criminals to lift me" on their way to the execution, and "they ordered me to lift their criminals" when the death sentence was carried out. Then the cross narrates what it *geseah* in its own grisly vision of events: "I saw the Lord of mankind hasten with great zeal because he wished to ascend onto me" and "I saw" the earth tremble (33–7). The cross not only speaks and sees, but it can act. Its anthropomorphizing extends even to its attitude toward its *cyning*, when it adopts the ethos of the loyal heroic thane who defends his lord to the death, but the cross must remain passive and check this impulse to act. Once the *Drihten* ascends the cross their relationship is changed in a way that somewhat resembles conversion or baptism but even more emphatically as the newly forged bonds of loyalty and love between a retainer and his lord. A chiastic line nicely captures how the gallows changes to a cross once it unites with Christ: *Rod wæs ic aræred; ahof ic ricne Cyning* (44), where the lack of a conjunction between the two half-lines prompts the reader to supply some kind of connection between the two, such as "I was raised a cross *after/because* I lifted the powerful king." Together Lord and thane become an object of scorn for the tormentors, and the cross feels the blood soaking its surface after "he had sent on his spirit" (49). Darkness covers the earth and all creation weeps. Christ is taken down and buried. The cross is eventually buried and later rescued by friends who decorate it with gold and silver (78).

After the defining act of the crucifixion the narrative turns to moralizing as the cross explains its unique significance to Christians, especially the help it can provide to humans as they face the prospect of their death and judgment. It also enjoins the dreamer to make this vision known to others (95–6). "No one needs to be afraid," it concludes, "who has been carrying on his breast [*or* within his breast] the best of signs" – *þe him ær in breostum bereð beacna selest* – because the cross helps the faithful to heaven (117–21). During the course of the vision the cross transforms itself in stages from a spectacle that fills the gaze of all creation, to the wooden gallows, to a warrior serving his Lord, to forgotten landfill, and finally (in the dreamer's description) to the humble sign worn around the neck or even carried internally as a mental image. It moves from the cosmic to the personal.

After the vision ends, the narrator has hopes of eternal life and is even eager for it: "Now my life's hope is that I alone may seek the cross of victory more often than all people, honor it well. Desire for that is great in my heart, and my protection is directed to the cross"

(126–31). The dreamer, having grown old, expects the cross to come fetch him to heaven, which is described in detail with a series of *þær is* passages about the particular kinds of *blis* in heaven (135–44), and the poem ends with a summary of the act of redemption *on þæm gealg-treowe* ("on the gallows-tree"), which freed sinners and gave them hope for salvation.

As a poem *The Dream of the Rood* constructs itself through a complex layering of perspectives, the first of which is the first person narrator who introduces and experiences the dream vision. The vision itself is the second. The next layer is the speaking cross, and finally there is the account of the crucifixion derived from the gospels, but even this is complicated by its adoption of the conventions of Germanic lordship, which are yet another layer. The poem's design keeps a tight control over them, however, so the question becomes: why such complexity? What does it enable? The biblical message of salvation is the poem's core message, to which the other layers provide an imaginative access, first through the familiar figure of a dreamer and then through the equally personable cross, which tells the familiar story of the crucifixion in a daringly affective way. The vision lends authority to the dream experience; the speaking cross personalizes the encounter; and the story it tells dramatizes an account that might otherwise seem foreign and distant. In moving through these layers to the central Christian mystery the dreamer is personally transformed in a way that the gospel story alone (apparently) cannot do.

As a genre the dream vision has ancient roots, with many examples from the Bible and from classical literature.[7] *The Dream of the Rood* adds features that make it stand out from other contemporary examples to which it might be compared, but all dream visions adopt a voice of authority from a world beyond the senses, which in this case is from the Christian otherworld. Given the hierarchical nature of religious authority in the medieval church, it may seem surprising that a poem like *The Dream* could arrogate to itself an authoritative stance, offering an alternative perspective on the crucifixion. Of course visions could always be suspect, and indeed the reason Hild assembled the scholars of Whitby was to test whether Cædmon's vision was from God or the devil. And the precise terms of their test is revealing, because a diabolical gift would not be able to turn sacred stories into such beautiful song. Dream visions, however, trace their legitimacy from the Bible, in which prophetic dreams seem to be a special subgenre, and they are given credibility by still other passages such as "The Lord came down in a pillar of the cloud, . . . He said to them: Hear my words: if there be among you a prophet of the Lord, I will appear to him in a vision, or I will speak to him in a dream" (Numbers 12:5–6). The last verse suggests that a dream vision *becomes* the proof of one's status as a prophet, analogous to the way that miracles demonstrate a saint's sanctity. In brief, a vision is a species of miracle.

Part of the complexity of *The Dream of the Rood* derives from the skillful fusion of two rhetorical tropes. One is *ekphrasis*, the literary description of a work of art, the most famous example of which may be the careful depiction of the shield of Achilles in book 18 of the *Iliad*. What makes ekphrasis different from other kinds of description is that it takes a visible artifact as its object (and not a person, for example, or an abstract concept or something from the natural world), so that it generates a double layering of literary art and visual art. In other words the physical features of the artifact are "seen" only through the poem's words. W. J. T. Mitchell succinctly defines this doubling as "the verbal representation of visual representation,"[8] but the insistence on visual *representation* goes a step too far because it implies that the artifacts themselves always have a mimetic function, which may not be the case. As an example consider the Old English riddle for an everyday implement, given here in the translation by Kevin Crossley-Holland:

> A strange object caught my eye, used to feed cattle
> by men of every town; it has many teeth
> and is useful to men as it scrapes around, its face
> to the ground. It plunders greedily, searching for plants
> along the grassy slopes, and brings them home;
> it always finds those which are not rooted firmly,
> but leaves the beautiful living flowers behind,
> quietly standing where they spring from the soil,
> brightly gleaming, blooming, growing.[9]

The answer to the riddle is a rake, a human artifact that does not represent anything else. By contrast, the riddle itself is entirely given over to verbal representation – even if it conceals as much as it reveals. (Riddles will be discussed in more detail in chapter 5.)

The second trope is the personification of an object that speaks about itself, known as prosopopoeia, which was a very common rhetorical device in Anglo-Saxon England (already encountered in the discussion on *The Husband's Message* in the first chapter). On a mundane level there are examples of jewelry and weapons with inscriptions that say "X owns me," as if the objects themselves utter the inscribed words, and the trope faintly operates in the expression "as books say to us," found in Cynewulf, *The Battle of Brunanburh*, and elsewhere. Another Old English riddle gives an extended example of prosopopoeia with striking similarities to *The Dream of the Rood*:

> I'm surrounded by flames and sport with the wind,
> I'm clothed with finery and the storm's great friend,
> ready to travel, but troubled by fire,
> a glade in full bloom and a burning flame;
> friends often pass me from hand to hand,
> and I'm kissed by ladies and courteous men.
> But when I raise myself, with reverence
> proud men must bow to me; I bring
> man's happiness to full maturity.[10]

The riddle's solution is wood in its various forms: a living tree, fuel for fire, perhaps a cup, and finally a cross demanding reverence and promising *eadignesse*, "happiness."

There is little doubt that Old English readers were alert to the play of rhetorical tropes in *The Dream of the Rood*. A large stone cross dating from the eighth century in the northern town of Ruthwell ingeniously collapses the distinction between prosopopoeia (the object speaking of itself) and ekphrasis (literary representation of an artifact) as they are dramatized in the poem.[11] A number of lines from the cross's speech are carved in runic letters around the Ruthwell Cross's edge, so that the stone cross mimics the speaking cross from the vision and "utters" its identity. However, the runic letters are at the same time ekphrastic in creating "a verbal representation of a visual representation" – in this case the very cross on which they are carved. (It is also a visual representation of a verbal representation – the reverse of ekphrasis – but at some point the degrees of representation can spiral out of control!). The quotation from *The Dream* is not exact, but beginning with line 39 it gives a foreshortened version of the cross's defining action: "Almighty God stripped himself when he wanted to ascend onto the gallows . . ." A number of the runic letters have been lost

A nineteenth-century engraving of the Ruthwell Cross in Dumfriesshire.
Note the runic letters on the outermost edge.

through damage (especially during the iconoclasm of the seventeenth century), but a second excerpt begins with words taken from line 56 of the poem, transliterated from the runes below in their Northumbrian dialect and without punctuation:

> + krist wæs on rodi
> hweþræ þer fusæ   fearran kwomu
> æþþilæ til anum   ic þæt al biheald
> (*Reader* lines 56–8)

Christ was on the cross; nevertheless eager noble ones came from afar to him in solitude. I beheld all that.

Yet another abbreviated excerpt from the poem appears on yet another cross, only this one is a specimen of metalwork known as the Brussel's Cross or the Drahmal Cross, because it is signed with the prosopopoeic inscription *Drahmal me worhte*, "Drahmal created me."[12] A silver strip around the edges contains an inscription (in Latin letters) which reads:

> Rod is min nama geo ic ricne cyning
> Bær byfigynde blode bestemed

Cross is my name. Long ago, trembling and soaked with blood I bore a powerful king.

The first line corresponds closely to line 44 of *The Dream* and the second may draw from the second half of line 48, but the quotation is short and loose enough that its relation to the longer poem is unclear. The inscription continues, in prose: "Æthelmær and his brother Athelwold ordered this cross made for the praise of Christ and the soul of their brother Ælfric." Whatever the relation between the Drahmal Cross's brief verse inscription and *The Dream of the Rood*, the personification of the physical object is yet another illustration that Anglo-Saxon audiences were alive to the rhetorical play of prosopopoeia.

In combining ekphrasis and prosopopoeia, *The Dream of the Rood* fashions a familiar yet complex system of signs for interpretation. Unlike the riddles, it does not misdirect the reader with opaque references but uses each trope to draw the dreamer (and reader) into a deeper spiritual understanding of the central act of Christianity. As an otherworldly vision, what the dreamer sees is at once a wooden gallows and an elaborately decorated crucifix – a product of carpenters and goldsmiths – but it miraculously shifts from one to the other as the dreamer sees drops of blood coalesce into gems. Moreover the cross has the miraculous ability to extend itself in time and space so that what started as a human artifact, a gallows, becomes unearthly. When it speaks to fashion its identity like a personified object in a riddle, it also adopts a spectrum of human memories and emotions, but even these are given divine approval by the cross's glorification. In placing itself so explicitly in the lord–thane relationship it both particularizes the heroic tradition (with the pronoun *ic*) and univer- salizes it in a way that ingeniously accommodates the pre-conversion Anglo-Saxon poetic tradition to the religious worldview of the Christian church.

The Pulpit

Uton we hycgan   hwær we ham agen
ond þonne geþencan   hu we þider cumen,
ond we þonne eac tilien   þæt we to moten
in þa ecan   eadignesse,
þær is lif gelong   in lufan Dryhtnes,
hyht in heofonum.   Þæs sy þam Halgan þonc
þæt he usic geweorþade,   wuldres Ealdor,
ece Dryhten,   in ealle tid.
                                        Amen.
                    (*The Seafarer*, Guide 117–24)

Let us ponder where we may possess a home and then think how we may go there, and then we should also strive that we may go into the eternal happiness where life, joy in the heavens, resides in the love of the Lord. Let there be thanks to the Holy One that he, the Ruler of glory, the eternal Lord, has honored us for all time.

The ending of *The Seafarer* has had a vexed reception history since the nineteenth century, when many scholars were convinced that the Christian moralizing beginning in the second half of the poem was grafted onto an earlier pre-Christian poem. Thus many editions up through the first half of the twentieth century omitted various segments from the latter part, and indeed the latest edition of *Sweet's Anglo-Saxon Reader* continues a decision made over 100 years ago to omit the final 16 lines, including the eight quoted above, so its readers today may be led to believe the poem ends with the pious, gnomic sentiments, "Happy is the one who lives humbly: mercy comes to him from the heavens. The Creator establishes that spirit in him, because he trusts in his power" (107–8), unless they carefully read the notes at the back of the book. Over the last 50 years, however, a consensus has emerged to approach the poem as thematically unified, especially after Dorothy Whitelock argued in 1950 that its central action is a pilgrimage or voluntary exile from one's native land for the love of God (*peregrinatio pro amore Dei*). The *peregrinatio* was an established literary theme (and ascetic practice) among early medieval Christians in the British Isles, an essential part of which involved the deliberate embrace of hardships in the hope of heavenly rewards.[1] Interpreted in light of this controlling metaphor, the poem moves from physical hardships on the seas through the pleasures renounced in favor of the life abroad and finally to the hoped-for heavenly rewards. The final eight lines emphasize the goal of the seafarer's voluntary exile, which is of course the eternal joys of the heavenly home. Even when it is accepted as a conceptually unified lyric, however, the poem's many ambiguous or problematic passages continue to provoke a wide range of interpretive responses.

The final "Amen" is not part of the poem proper because it falls outside the metrical limits of the line, but it shows that at least one medieval reader accepted the poem's closing as part of a distinct religious discourse – specifically as the kind delivered by a homilist. It is not the "Amen" that gives away its homiletic tone but the first word of the quoted passage, *uton*, which has been classified by one editor as a "hortatory auxiliary."[2] Etymologically it derives from the subjunctive form of a common verb meaning "to go" (*witan*) and translates literally as a first person plural: "let's go." But the Anglo-Saxons began to construe *uton* (or *wuton*) as a separate word as its original meaning dissipated and it was used to inject a mood of exhortation ("let us"), construed with the infinitive of a clause. In other words *uton* shifted from a lexical verb to an auxiliary (while the original verb *witan* continued as before). Beyond the tradeoff between semantics and syntax, however, *uton* came to signal the conventional closing of a homily, in which the preacher drove home the moral of his exposition, and a receptive audience might respond "Amen." The sense of hopeful expectation is reinforced by the repeated use of the subjunctive mood in the verbs *agen, cumen, tilien, moten,* usually translated into modern English with a phrasing that includes "may" or "should," or even "let us."

The association between the hortatory auxiliary *uton* and homiletic endings is strong but not absolute. The word appears in other contexts, as in *Beowulf*: "Arise, protector of the people, let us quickly go" (*uton . . . feran*, 1390) and even in God's words of creation, "Let us make mankind in our image" (*Uton . . . wircean*). But it is far more common in homilies and in other religious literature with a marked hortatory function, such as saints' lives. *The Seafarer* is not alone among poems to dip into the verbal register of homilies to elevate its closing lines; *The Fates of the Apostles* likewise ends "Let us cry out more earnestly to God" (*utu . . . cleopigan, Anthology*, line 115). The audiences of such passages were likely conditioned from a lifetime of listening to homilies to expect a preacher's closing exhortation after the initial *uton*. Readers of *The Fates* would find the poem literally surrounded by homiletic context because its manuscript, the Vercelli Book, contains 23 prose items of such material.

The anonymous author of the tenth homily in the Vercelli Book recasts his Latin sources to create a vivid exposition on the importance of repentance before the individual Christian's day of judgment. Like *The Seafarer*, *Vercelli Homily X* ends with an exhortation to turn to the better things of the Lord – *Utan we þænne wendan to þam beteran* (*Anthology* p. 106, line 196) – and it locates the heavenly home in the "there" of heaven, where *þær* is repeated so often it almost signifies a physical place. The homily begins with a gentle reminder of the incarnation and teaching mission of Christ, which grants the heavenly kingdom to the virtuous. An interesting list of sins to avoid includes the usual suspects – hypocrisy, murder, lies, theft, blasphemy, and anger – but it also includes sorcery, incantation, and evil witchcraft (*scin-cræft, galdor-sang, unriht lyb-lac*) (lines 33–9).

In a passage that bristles with words of judgment, including the verb *deman*, "to judge," and the noun *dom*, "judgment, law," the Devil demands that sinners be held to the letter of the law. Like an aggressive prosecuting attorney he takes pains to point out the inflexible law that requires sinners to be consigned to hell. He flatters Christ as the Judge by pointing out (correctly) how he died on the cross to save humankind, and there is even an appeal to egalitarian principles in the way that all people, even kings, are brought down to the same abject level at the moment of justice. In one particularly arresting image the Devil describes his temptations as a kind of anti-David, a harpist to whose enticing music the sinners came running. Christ in effect upholds the Devil's legal interpretation, because he shows no mercy to the sinners and condemns them to hell: *bið se Dema þearl*, "the Judge is severe" (48–81). Much of the remainder of the homily addresses the particular evil of wealthy people hoarding wealth and the blessedness of the needy. There is an insistent inversion: the greater the honor, the worse the humiliation; the greater the wealth, the worse the punishment. Wealth is not something earned by the rich but a gift from God that comes with an additional share of Christian responsibility, summed up in the tight chiastic constructions: *Þam þe Dryhten mycel syleð, myceles he hine eac eft manað. Þam þe he micel to forlæteð, mycel he to þam seceð*; "To those whom the Lord grants much, much will he demand in return. To those whom he allowed much, much will he seek for it" (p. 104, lines 149–50).

From the powerful denunciation of miserliness, the homily turns to the more general theme of earthly transience, using language that resembles the famous passage in *The Wanderer*:

Hwær syndon þa rican caseras and cyningas þa þe gio wæron, oððe þa cyningas þe we io cuðon? Hwær syndon þa ealdormen þa þe bebodu setton? Hwær is demera domstow? Hwær is hira ofermetto, butan mid moldan beþeahte and in witu gecyrred? . . . Hwær coman middangeardes gestreon? Hwær com worulde wela? Hwær cwom foldan fægernes? Hwær coman þa þe geornlicost æhta tiledon and oðrum eft yrfe læfdon? Swa læne is sio oferlufu eorðan gestreona: emne hit bið gelice rena scurum, þonne he of heofenum swiðost dreoseð and eft hraðe eal toglideð; bið fæger weder and beorht sunne. Swa tealte syndon eorðan dreamas, and swa todæleð lic and sawle. Þonne is us uncuð hu se Dema ymb þæt gedon wylle. (*Anthology* p. 104, 173–82)

Where are the powerful emperors and kings who formerly existed, or the kings we once knew? Where are the noblemen who set the laws? Where is the hall of justice? Where is their haughtiness except covered with dirt and turned into punishments? . . . Where has the earth's treasure gone? Where has the world's wealth gone? Where has the land's beauty gone? Where have they gone who most zealously sought possessions and left them as an inheritance for others? Thus the obsession with earthly treasures is transitory: it is just like a rain-shower when it falls heaviest from the heavens and later flows completely away; it will be fair weather and bright sun. Thus the earth's joys are precarious, and thus the body separates from the soul. Then it will be unknown to us how the Judge will decide it.

In this rhetorical tour de force the catalogues consign all the splendors of the earth to oblivion in a way that makes the lesson universal, even though the sharpest criticism is directed toward the wealthy and powerful. If their glory is transitory, then so is that of the rest of us, as the simile of the rain-shower makes clear in its elegant simplicity. The theme of earthly justice at the beginning turns to divine justice at the end. In the next section the Lord speaks, promising mercy to those who love him and do penance, and continues with a paraphrase of Matthew 16:26: "For what doth it profit a man, if he gain the whole world and suffer the loss of his own soul?" The homily then ends with the *Utan we* exhortation promising the joys of heaven where the Lord "lives and reigns with all the saints forever. Amen" (204–5).

Vercelli Homily X is one of 23 anonymous Old English homilies in the Vercelli Book, a miscellany compiled in the middle of the second half of the tenth century, which also included *The Fates, The Dream of the Rood*, and four other poems. Another 19 homilies are found in a slightly later collection called *The Blickling Homilies*, and dozens more are contained in manuscripts dating from the tenth to the twelfth centuries.[3] Throughout this discussion the term "homily" has been used in a loose sense, meaning any prose item with homiletic material suitable for delivery from the pulpit. However, in the strictest sense the word homily is reserved only for an exposition of the "pericope," that is, the biblical passages assigned to be read during the liturgy on a given day. The term "sermon" is reserved for other kinds of preaching, which could range widely in subject matter from, say, the Antichrist, to the sin of greed, to a saint's life. Indeed many items that are customarily counted among the homilies are clearly saints' lives with a formal opening and closing added to them. Because it is not clear that the Anglo-Saxons themselves distinguished between the two kinds of preaching, the following discussion will continue to use "homily" in the general sense.

After Ælfric was installed as a priest and monk at Cerne Abbas around 987, he turned his attention to vernacular homilies. He approached the project systematically and before long, with the help of his distinctive rhythmic prose, transformed the genre. Expanding on the example of earlier anonymous texts, he planned a collection that was more comprehensive and would avoid the heresy (*gedwyld*) that he found in many English books. His First Series of 40 homilies, however, was initially for use in his own monastery, which served as the

An early manuscript of Ælfric's *Homily on Ascension Sunday* in the First Series, which shows corrections entered in his own hand on the bottom of MS Royal 7 c.xii, folio 105r. British Library, London.

local parish church in that area of Dorset. If the congregation consisted of monks alone (as seems to be the case in many monasteries) there would be little reason to go to the trouble of making Old English homilies, since the monks knew Latin, and extensive homiliaries were already available in that language. But the local people around Cerne Abbas needed to hear preaching in "just plain English" like laypeople elsewhere in England.[4] Within seven years Ælfric expanded his project and issued two series of 40 homilies each, the *Catholic Homilies*, which were circulated throughout England as an ample and reliably orthodox body of preaching material. And he did not stop there. In addition to the two series, there are approximately another 50 homilies attributed to him.

Ælfric's *Homily on the Nativity of the Innocents* from the First Series offers a typical example of his technique. He bases it on the gospel story of Herod's murder of infants after the birth of Jesus, from Matthew 2:13–18, which was the reading assigned for the feast of the Holy Innocents on December 28. Because the gospel was read in Latin during the liturgy, Ælfric begins with a paraphrase, but he reaches back to include the entire story of Herod and the wise men from earlier verses in Matthew 2. He also supplements it with commentary drawn from at least seven sources to explain, for example, Herod's position under the Roman emperor and why he waited for two years before ordering the slaughter. A short passage illustrates his didactic approach. It begins with a paraphrase of Matthew 2:18, which is itself a quotation from Jeremiah 31:15, given some historical context and expounded by Ælfric:

> The gospel says that Rachel lamented her children and did not wish to be comforted, because they were no more. She was called Rachel the wife of the patriarch Jacob, and she symbolized God's congregation, which laments its spiritual child; but she does not wish to be comforted that they might return to the worldly struggle who once conquered the earth with victorious death and escaped its miseries to a glorious crowning with Christ. (*Reader* p. 73, lines 128–34)

Building on the fourfold method of exegesis, this brief passage moves from the literal, to the historical (Rachel as Jacob's wife), to the anagogical (the souls who are saved through Christ). The larger lessons of the homily, however, concern the ghastly punishments reserved for Herod in this life and the next, in contrast to Christ's young warriors (*his geongan cempan*) and innocent martyrs (*unscæððige martyras*) who were able to suffer death for his sake. Ælfric uses a series of rhetorical contrasts to aestheticize and give spiritual signification to the slaughter, thus keeping the potential bathos of innocent suffering in check: although they were too young to profess Christ, they suffered for him; they were witnesses, although they did not know him yet; their birth was blessed because they were able to die into eternal life; they were seized from their mothers' breasts to be thrust into angelic bosoms; such criminal wickedness only did them a great favor (109–15). "They are called blossoms of martyrs [*martyra blostman*] because they were just like sprouting blossoms in the middle of the cold of unbelief, as if withered by a certain frost of persecution" (115–18).

Ælfric's homily for Septuagesima Sunday (the third Sunday before Lent) is another good example of an exposition of the gospel passage for the day's liturgy, in this case the well-known Parable of the Vineyard from Matthew 20:1–16. After paraphrasing the story, he cites his main source, St Gregory, to give a short commentary. The vineyard's owner is God; the vines are God's chosen, from Abel to the end of the world; and the workers are prophets and teachers to guide the people by cutting away the misshapen branches (*þa misweaxendan bogas, Reader* p. 62, line 55). The hours of the day when different groups are hired correspond to the ages of the world: the early morning from Adam to Noah, the third hour from Noah to Abraham, the sixth hour from Abraham to Moses, and the ninth hour from Moses to the coming of Christ. The eleventh hour lasts until the end of the world, so it includes the audience's present time and raises the question of unbelievers who live in the age when conversion to Christianity is possible, but not universal:

Truly at the eleventh hour the heathen were called and it was said to them, "Why do you stand here idle all day?" The heathen stood idle all day because they neglected the labor of eternal life for such a long period on the earth. But understand how they answered the lord of the vineyard: "Because no one hired us." Truly there was no patriarch or prophet sent to the heathen people who might censure their error before the coming of Christ through his incarnation. What does it mean that no one hired us in the vineyard, except that no one preached to us the way of life? (pp. 63–4, lines 76–87)

The use of "us" in the last lines is interesting, because in both instances it is not a quotation, but part of a paraphrase for "no one hired us" (following Gregory's homily). But because Ælfric's audience is living in the last age, the distance between "we" from the parable and "we" in the congregation can collapse. Ælfric calls the eleventh-hour workers *hæþen*, a word that in his homilies generally means "unbeliever, heathen" but in this vernacular context would extend to include the *hæþene* Anglo-Saxons before God's "way of life" was preached to them. As if to make the connection more apparent, Ælfric repeats *hæþen* three times, translating a single instance of Gregory's *gentiles*. It is another thread linking the parable to the "we" of Ælfric's audience, who as believers are now employed in the vineyard and who have no excuse (*beladung*), and whose heathen ancestors were less fortunate though less culpable because "no one hired us."

Ælfric offers another interpretation of the intervals of the day when the workers were hired, which correspond to the stages in personal growth from infancy to old age, and at each stage individuals may be led to virtue and a just life (p. 64, lines 90–105). While Ælfric closely follows Gregory's homily, some of his changes show his willingness to balance one authoritative source against another. The parable from Matthew ends "For many are called, but few are chosen," which the source homily by Gregory the Great interprets in a literal way: salvation is reserved for very few. But Ælfric instead (and disarmingly) cites another homily by Gregory to support the assertion that the number of God's chosen warriors (*ða gecorenan Godes cempan*, p. 67, line 189) will be great enough to fill the myriad thrones abandoned by Lucifer and his legions. Some have seen in this modification and others a tendency for Ælfric to emphasize personal merit at the expense of grace. His closing exhortation, for example, urges his audience to repent their sins and emphasizes the reciprocal relation between God's mercy and the individual's good will: "He prepares our good will as a help, and he helps our prepared will, who lives and reigns now and forever. Amen" (p. 68, lines 228–30).[5]

One of the important lessons of the parable of the vineyard is that preachers like Ælfric are obliged to tend the vines, that is, to guide the people with orthodox teaching. It is a heavy obligation, and in the case of the Bible fraught with dangers, because while some passages were relatively straightforward, others especially in the Old Testament required careful explanation. From its earliest years Christianity had developed a complex system of exegesis to interpret the Bible (see the discussion in chapter 2), sometimes reconciling conflicting passages, for example, or finding orthodox signification in condemned practices like incest and child sacrifice. Yet exegetical interpretation (sometimes called typology) could be applied just as effectively in unobjectionable passages from the Bible, and Ælfric's homilies provide many kinds of examples.

What happens when exegetical interpretations are unavailable? On one occasion Ælfric's patron, the ealdorman Æthelwærd, asked him to translate the book of Genesis. He dutifully complied, but in a lengthy preface he explained why he felt dangerously vulnerable in doing so. A preacher or scholar can control the interpretation by using the exegetical method, but a translation of the Bible made the unglossed text available for erroneous readings by the unlearned. Ælfric relates a personal anecdote about his first Latin teacher, a semi-literate priest who read that the patriarch Jacob "had four wives – two sisters and their two servants" but who had no idea how to reconcile the difference between the old law and the new (*Guide* p. 191, lines 12–18). Such people with only a little learning cannot perceive the spiritual sense (*gastlice andgit*, p. 192, line 27), by which Ælfric means "how the old law was a foreshadowing of future things," or how the New Testament was the fulfillment of the Old (28–9). In one explanation of this *getacnung*, he points out how in the Book of Genesis God creates humankind "in our likeness" (*to ure anlicnisse*, p. 193, line 68), where the plural pronoun signifies the Trinity long before Christianity revealed the truth of the doctrine. The Preface ends with an anxious plea for future copyists not to introduce errors, which might lead to yet more heresy, and then who would be held accountable for that sin before God? Ælfric's anxiety was not directed only to readings of the Old Testament, because a prayer appended to the Second Series of his *Catholic Homilies* says, "Henceforth I will never translate the gospel or gospel commentaries from Latin into English" (*Ælfric* p. 114, lines 5–6). Despite – or because of – his misgivings, his translation of Genesis reduces the chance of unwitting error by inserting short explanatory glosses into the narrative and omitting some of the more egregious instances of forbidden practices.

A topic that colors and indeed motivates much of the homiletic writings in the decades around the year 1000 was speculation on the imminence of the Last Judgment. The topic itself was nothing new, because from its earliest years Christianity had supported a belief among some of the faithful that the Second Coming of Jesus was just around the corner. The last book of the New Testament, the Apocalypse (now known as the Book of Revelation, a less alarmist name), prophesies about the portents in such highly charged but ambiguous language that anyone looking into it with the right frame of mind can discover signs of impending doom. The year 1000 had special significance because of one passage:

> Blessed and holy is he that hath part in the first resurrection. In these the second death hath no power; but they shall be priests of God and of Christ; and shall reign with him a thousand years. And when the thousand years shall be finished, Satan shall be loosed out of his prison, and shall go forth, and shall seduce the nations, which are over the four quarters of the earth, Gog, and Magog, and shall gather them together to battle, the number of whom is as the sand of the sea. (20:6–7)

Because each of the seven ages of history was thought to number 1,000 years, Ælfric's contemporaries saw themselves living near the end of the age begun by the "first resurrection" of Christ, and they were thus facing the prospect of Satan "loosed out of his prison." Even though orthodox teaching consistently warned the faithful against attaching absolute significance to the number, some writers found the symbolic precision of 1,000 too compelling to ignore. It was a perfect number, as Augustine, Abbo of Fleury, and others commented (ten multiplied by itself three times). For example, one of the Blickling Homilies, written to be delivered on Holy Thursday, quotes a passage from the gospel of Luke that warns against predicting the exact time the world will end. "Nevertheless," it goes on to say in spite of this cautionary note,

> we know that it is not far off, because all the signs and foreshadowings that our Lord had predicted would come before Doomsday have all occurred except one alone, which is the accursed stranger, Antichrist, who has still not come to the earth. Yet it is not far when that will also occur; because this earth must necessarily come to an end in this age which is now present, for five of the [signs] have appeared in this age when this world must come to an end; and the greatest part of it has elapsed, exactly nine hundred and seventy-one years, in this year.[6]

The explicit reference to the year 971 makes this one of the better-known passages in the Blickling Homilies, because of its obvious relevance to dating the collection. But the writer's invocation of the year is fascinating for a different set of reasons, reasons that have more to do with the overt topic of this passage – whether one can know the date of the Last Judgment or not. The homily goes on to qualify this calculation by pointing out that the historical intervals are not exactly 1,000 years long: some are shorter, and others consist of as many as 3,000 years. Adding to the uncertainty is that even if there is an exact interval of 1,000 years, it is not clear whether the counting should begin from the birth of Christ or his death 33 years later. Yet the fascination takes hold, so that even after making its prudent concessions to orthodoxy, the homily still presses ahead with its prediction: because the year 1000 is approaching, *hit nis no feor* to Doomsday.

This contradiction, given in such a plainspoken way in this Blickling Homily, lies at the heart of much homiletic writing around the year 1000. Most use more subtlety in balancing assertions of the end of the world with qualifications on its unknowability, but the same tension characterizes the rhetoric of the more interesting writing. A telltale sign of millennialist writing, even when it is muted in other respects, is what I call the language of imminence. It includes words indicating an impending action, such as the adverb *gehende*, "near," or the verb *genealacan*, "to approach, draw near," or any number of phrases indicating a brief interval that situates itself in the present and anticipates the immediate future. It is not the same as saying the future is unknowable, which is a commonplace. One of the first things students of Old English learn is that the language can use the present tense to indicate future action where Modern English uses *will* in a verb phrase. So when Ælfric writes *cymð se Antecrist* it can mean "the Antichrist will come" (as it is usually translated) or "the Antichrist comes" or even "is coming." Thus something as simple as a verb tense allows Old English writers room for rhetorical play in the space between the present and the imminent future, and between what is and is not orthodox.

Ælfric's millennialist expectations changed radically in the few years between the publication of his First and Second Series of *Catholic Homilies*. The preface to his First Series sets the entire collection in an apocalyptic framework. It speaks of "this time which is the end of this world" (*þe is geendung þyssere worulde*, *Anthology* p. 116, line 12) and goes on to describe the reign of Antichrist in great detail for more than half of its total length. In a homily for the Ascension from the first series, Ælfric writes, "We see that the end is very near, though it is unknown to us."[7] The final homily in the series, for the second Sunday of Advent, discusses signs that foretell the impending end of the world, based on the well-known apocalyptic passage from Luke 21:25–8:

> And there shall be signs in the sun, and in the moon, and in the stars; and upon the earth distress of nations, by reason of the confusion of the roaring of the sea and of the waves; Men withering away for fear, and expectation of what shall come upon the whole world. For the powers of heaven shall be moved; And then they shall see the Son of man coming in a cloud, with great power and majesty. But when these things begin to come to pass, look up, and lift up your heads, because your redemption is at hand.

Ælfric tells us that some of these signs have been fulfilled, and others are feared in the future, in anticipation of *his genealæcendan dom*, "his approaching judgment." The savior says your salvation approaches (p. 526, line 76); a prophet says the great day of judgment *is swiðe gehende* ("is very near," p. 530, lines 169 and 180). Ælfric, however, is careful to put these prophecies into the mouths of Christ and prophets. And he even reinterprets them so that imminence is no longer the point. "Even if it were yet another thousand years to that day," he writes, "it would not be far off, because whatever ends will be short and quick and will be as if it had never been, when it has ended" (p. 530, lines 180–3). This twist is another technique for having it both ways: on the one hand he plants the idea that the end is near, especially by using the words of impeccably divine authorities, but on the other hand he is too cautious to venture such a judgment himself. He redefines imminence, because the redemption that Luke proclaims is "at hand" can stretch out to another thousand years in Ælfric's scheme, which is nevertheless a short time.

Even this caution was finally not enough for Ælfric, because in his Second Series of homilies he entirely avoids speculation about the end of the world. After 994 whenever he discusses the last things, it is as exegetical exposition, with no reference to a time when they might come about. Some have traced this shift to Ælfric's increasing

preoccupation with the Viking invasions, which had become a formidable threat over his lifetime, and indeed within a few years after
Ælfric's death the King of Denmark, Swein Forkbeard, became the ruler
of all England (1013–14) and was shortly followed by his son Cnut
(1016–35). In considering the problem of the invading armies in
light of God's plan for the Anglo-Saxon church, Ælfric could give it
two Christian "readings": he could interpret the Vikings as instruments
of divine wrath directed against the sinful Christians in England, or he
could interpret the invasion on a universal scale as one of the signs
foretelling the end of the world. Early in their careers, Ælfric and
Wulfstan tended to combine both possibilities so that while the Vikings
were instruments of divine wrath, they were also harbingers of Doomsday. But there is a logical inconsistency here. The terrible events
preceding the Last Judgment are foreordained for everyone (according
to the Bible) and are not designed to punish any particular group,
such as backsliding Anglo-Saxons.

By the time he wrote the Second Series (994), Ælfric removed
apocalypticism from his thinking about the Vikings and urged resistance
for less specific reasons. The invasions no longer portend the end of
the world, nor are they punishments, but instead are absorbed into a
comprehensive struggle between the forces of good and evil, between
God and the Devil. Christians should resist the Vikings as they should
resist any other threat to their religion. Reinterpreting the invasions
in terms of this age-old conflict, however, does not necessarily exclude
apocalypticism. That is, there can be a sense that Christians should
resist the heathens *and* that the end is around the corner. There is just
no cause-and-effect relation between the two.

However, Ælfric may have dropped apocalypticism for another
reason. There is a fine line between convincing people that the end is
near and convincing them that the end will come at a specific time.
Church authorities such as Augustine, Gregory, Isidore, and Bede were
adamant in discouraging speculation about the precise date of the
Last Judgment, and Ælfric was careful to caution in his own writings
that no one can predict when the end will come about. Even so, he
cultivated an interest in the ages of history, which found its way into
his homilies. And he was convinced that he was living at the end of
the last age.[8] By 994 Ælfric may have been concerned that his earlier
eschatological homilies would contribute to irresponsible speculation
about the year 1000 as the precise date for the Second Coming,

just as he was anxious about unintended consequences of his biblical translations.

For those who prophesy the end of the world, keeping the exact date obscure or even approximate offers a rhetorical advantage, as Gregory the Great realized when he observed, "The more we are unable to foreknow when it will come the more it ought to be feared as always arriving." As pope, Gregory exploited the rhetorical potential of such fear in his letter to King Æthelberht (d. 616) when he urged that the signs of raging pestilence, earthquakes, famines, and celestial portents all around him in Rome pointed to the imminent end of the world.[9] Therefore, he concludes, King Æthelberht and his people should convert and prepare their souls for the Last Judgment. Ælfric and other homilists likewise took advantage of the persuasive potential of this uncertainty and fear, even though it bordered on a contradiction: it will happen any day now, but no one knows when it will happen. Imminence had the advantage of being perfectly orthodox, yet an effective rhetorical stick for beating the faithful into repentance and moral behavior.

Archbishop Wulfstan's embrace of millennialism stands in sharp contrast to Ælfric's efforts finally to keep it at arm's length. His best-known example of the rhetoric of imminence is his *Sermon to the English People* (1014), which in its opening sentence makes a stark assertion about the nearness of the Last Judgment: "Beloved people, learn what the truth is: this world is in haste, and it approaches the end [*hit nealæcð þam ende*], and thus the longer the world goes on the worse it gets, and it must necessarily grow much worse because of the people's sin before the coming of Antichrist, and indeed it is becoming terrifying and horrible throughout the world" (*Reader* pp. 85–6, lines 1–5). Even the Latin title found on several manuscripts draws attention to the correlation between the Viking depredations and the year. It reads *Sermo Lupi ad Anglos*, or "Sermon of Wulf to the English," and continues "when the Danes were most grievously persecuting them, which was in the year 1014 from the birth of Our Lord Jesus Christ." Less well known are his other eschatological homilies from around the year 1000, which repeat similar themes: the time of Antichrist is *swiðe gehende* ("very near") and Judgment Day *georne nealæcð* ("quickly approaches"). Such sentiments are so pervasive, in fact, that the theme of Antichrist has been called "the theological preoccupation of Wulfstan at the beginning of his career."[10] In later years he modified his references to the Last Judgment to make them more didactic than prophetic. Never merely a theme or a motif, however, Wulfstan's invocation of Antichrist and the Last Judgment enabled him to employ the language of imminence to give these homilies a lapel-grabbing urgency that we might find disconcerting today, but which would be compelling to the right audience, on the right occasion, delivered by the right speaker.

Wulfstan cultivated a prose style that like Ælfric's made use of alliteration, rhyme, and rhythmic phrases, but his is quite distinctive. The following passage from his *Sermon to the English*, which is one of several such lists of atrocities committed by the English people, is lineated to gather his characteristic doublets to the left margin:

> Ne dohte hit nu lange
> inne ne ute, ac wæs
> here and hunger,
> bryne and blodgyte on gewelhwylcran ende
> oft and gelome; and us
> stalu and cwalu,
> stric and steorfa,
> orfcwealm and uncoþu,
> hol and hete
> and rypera reaflac derede swyþe þearle,
> and ungylda swyðe gedrehtan,
> and us unwedera foroft weoldan unwæstma.
>
> (51–6)

Nothing has prospered now for a long time within and abroad, but there has very often been devastation and hunger, burning and bloodshed in every district; and theft and murder, plague and pestilence, cattle-plague and disease, envy and hatred and theft by plunderers have harmed us excessively, and excessive taxes have greatly afflicted us, and disastrous weather very often has caused us crop failure.

Printing the doublets as a column gives a visual impact of their prevalence, but in oral delivery their primary effectiveness would be as a memorable rhythmic unit and thus it is unimportant that some of them are tautologies. They also make use of rhyme (*stalu and cwalu*) and even more frequently alliteration (*stric and steorfa*). Like the *Beowulf*-poet, Wulfstan is fond of the negative prefix *un-*, as in *ungylda*, *unwedera*, and *unwæstma*, in which a coinage like *un-wæstma* works by positing the root meaning "fruit, crop, growth" and negating it. Here *unweder* and *unwæstm* make a rhetorically effective pairing because they reproduce on a verbal level the large-scale calamity described by Wulfstan, where disastrous weather causes disastrous crops, but *wæstm* and *weder* leave their own trace to remind the audience of the proper state of affairs. A final feature of Wulfstan's style that deserves comment is his liberal use of intensifiers such as *swyþe þearle*, "very severely," and *oft and gelome* and *foroft*, "very often" – but many are hard to translate, because in this passage the first literally means "greatly severely" and the second "often and often." These and other intensifiers appear in varying combinations: *oft*, for example, comes as the comparative *oftor* and superlative *oftost*, which are similar to *ealles to gelome*, "very often." He also uses *georne*, "very, earnestly, quickly," *to*, "too," *micle*, "greatly," and *eall* in various forms. Taken in isolation on the page, the features of Wulfstan's style may seem overly contrived, but it helps to remember he composed it for oral delivery, where the cadences, sound play, and repetition could hold the congregation's attention while the pastoral message hit home. The cumulative effect of the rhetorical pyrotechnics in the passage above gives the impression of disaster overwhelming England, whatever the historical reality may have been.

It is not necessary to think that Wulfstan really believed that the end was just around the corner as long as it served his agenda for social and moral reform throughout England, though this is perhaps too cynical a view. But it does seem that part of his interest was motivated by its hortatory usefulness in getting the faithful to mend their sinful ways. The *Sermon to the English* is well known for the way it itemizes the atrocities that Wulfstan claims to have witnessed in England: adultery, fornication, rape, theft, witches, valkyries, the desecration of churches, backstabbing, pledge-breaking, and so on. The sins of the English are about as heinous as those of the Vikings. But because they are Christians their behavior has earned divine wrath in the form of the Vikings, whom God allows to inflict even more atrocities. At times Wulfstan associates the Vikings with Antichrist because of their inhuman viciousness, but at other times they are instruments of God's punishment, and occasionally even unlikely models of admirable behavior, as for example in their respectful treatment of shrines to their pagan gods. The Anglo-Saxons, who as Christians should know better and are thus more culpable, have committed their worst crimes not against their pagan adversaries, but against one another.

Wulfstan does not, as one might expect, end his homily with rousing prophetic visions of the arrival of Antichrist or the Second Coming. Instead, he shifts the perspective entirely and adopts a providential view of world history that he cites from Gildas, the sixth-century author of *De Excidio Britanniae*, "*On the Ruin of Britain*." Rather than organizing history according to the framework of the "Seven Ages," Gildas proposed a cyclical model. God's faithful enjoy peace and prosperity as long as they observe his laws, but when they grow degenerate they are punished by their own wickedness and by the invasion of less worthy people – pagans, in this case – who might later become the next recipients of God's favor. This model guided Gildas's interpretation of the invasion of the Angles and Saxons in the fifth century, who came as pagan scourges for the degenerate Britons, eventually subdued them, were given dominion over the island, and later were converted to Christianity. Eventually the Anglo-Saxons assumed the role of the new favored people on the island of Britain.

Wulfstan's conclusion neither hints that the end of the world is around the corner (as mentioned above) nor declares that the historical cycle has run its course for the Anglo-Saxons (as one might expect). Instead it urges the English to mend their ways. It is not, after all, too late. The final sentences have five separate *utan* exhortations urging the audience to reform, because "we know of worse deeds among the English than we ever heard anywhere among the British" (p. 92, lines 187–8). After invoking the earlier example of the British as a warning, the exhortations move in turn to human justice, the love of God and his laws, keeping one's word and other personal virtues, and finally a comprehensive call to prepare for the final judgment (186– 202). The last exhortation reads:

[A]nd utan gelome understandan þone miclan dom þe we ealle to sculon, and beorgan us georne wið þone weallendan bryne helle wites, and geearnian us þa mærþa and þa myrhða þe God hæfð gegearwod þam þe his willan on worolde gewyrcað. God ure helpe. Amen (pp. 92– 3, lines 197–202)

And let us often understand the great judgment we all must meet, and save ourselves against the welling fire of hell's punishment, and obtain the glory and mirth which God has prepared for those who do his will on earth. May God help us. Amen.

The syntactic balance among the main clauses underscores the causal progression they trace: understanding leads to protection from hell, which leads to gaining heaven. And there is an interesting interplay between sound and sense in, for example, the assonance between *geearnian* and *gegearwod*, and the alliteration-assonance of *mærþa* and *myrhða*, and the final alliteration of *willan on worolde gewyrcað*. After castigating his audience for most of the homily, Wulfstan resurrects their hope by holding out the possibility that virtuous living will alleviate God's wrath and remove the Viking menace, bringing about a time of peace and prosperity again.

The discussion so far has spoken of Wulfstan only as a homilist, but from the time he became bishop of London in 996 he was also active in affairs of state. In the year 1002 he became bishop of York and of Worcester (holding both offices simultaneously), and by 1008 he was writing a lawcode for King Æthelstan, the first of several such codes. Before Wulfstan turned his hand to the task a typical Anglo-Saxon legal clause might read:

> And let every moneyer whom one accuses of striking false coin since it was forbidden go to the threefold ordeal; if he be guilty, let him be slain.

The legal action is straightforward, the style analytical. The punishment follows the crime with the same inexorable logic as characterizes the vernacular lawcodes back to the early seventh century. But the equivalent law written by Wulfstan in Æthelred's code of 1008 reads:

> And let everyone shun deceitful deeds and loathsome abuses, that is false weights and wrong measures . . . and let one be eager for the improvement of the peace and for the improvement of money everywhere in the land.

It now sounds like a tract of Christian morals, full of judgmental adjectives like "deceitful" and "loathsome." The voice of the homilist is heard in the hortatory phrases "let everyone shun" and "let one be eager." But what is most unlike earlier lawcodes is the removal of the punishment-to-crime structure. How could a secular law rely so heavily on calls for general "improvement"? "It is as though," observes Patrick Wormald, "the Brandenburg concertos had been reorchestrated by Bruckner."[11] Later codes written by Wulfstan reinstated the specific penalties for offences, but the hortatory and ecclesiastical features remained.

No less remarkable than his legal prose is the fact that Wulfstan continued in his role of law-writer even after Cnut became king in 1016. Cnut's father Swein was one of the Vikings whose behavior so horrified Wulfstan in his *Sermon to the English*. However much Wulfstan associated the Danes with the Antichrist in earlier years, the newly crowned Cnut apparently won him over with his vigorous support of the church. Shortly after assuming the throne, Cnut retained Wulfstan again as a law-writer, and their collaboration culminated in the great code issued from Winchester at Christmas during 1020 or 1021.

More than a rhetorical exercise in applying his resonant homiletic style to the astringent language of law, Wulfstan's agenda seems to be one of sweeping moral reform. Crimes no doubt were always categorized as sins, but now the equivalence is made explicit. If the millenarian themes motivate Wulfstan's recasting of the lawcodes, they are curiously muted. Their relative absence may reflect the incompatibility of apocalyptic upheaval with the interests of political regimes. It can be a risky move for any government to encourage its people to think that the end of the world, and thus of civil society, is impending. The language of imminence can be volatile, inspiring moral reform in some societies but anarchy in others. Æthelstan and Cnut for different reasons were desperate to promote stability in their kingdom, a stability that would not be helped by lawcodes that trumpeted their own impending obsolescence. To the extent that Wulfstan's *Sermon to the English* reinforced associations between the Danes and the signs of the end, more such rhetoric could only be counterproductive to political stability after Cnut became king. What remained of Wulfstan's eschatology in the later laws were exhortations to moral reform without the prophetic voice that the end was near.

The Scholar

Saintly scholars such as Thomas Aquinas and Albert the Great occupy the brilliant sphere of the sun in Dante's *Paradiso*, and among the other inhabitants Beatrice singles out the "glowing breath" of Isidore of Seville, Bede, and Richard of Saint Victor (*Canto* X). Isidore (d. 636) was an enormously influential encyclopedist, and Richard (d. 1173) was a mystical theologian. But how does Bede deserve a place in paradise with the most venerated theologians known to Dante?

In the context of Old English studies, Bede is generally encountered through the vernacular translation of his Latin *Historia Ecclesiastica Gentis Anglorum* (731), and indeed episodes from it such as *Cædmon's Hymn* and King Edwin's conversion have been encountered in previous chapters of this book.[1] But throughout western Europe the name of Bede was also associated with his more overtly theological writings. An epilogue he added to the end of his *Ecclesiastical History* lists some 30 books he wrote over his career, and among these are pedagogical works (on grammar, metrics, etc.), saints' lives, and commentaries on various books of the Bible. His biblical exegeses were probably his main qualification for Dante's paradise, and like his other writings are characterized by deep learning, a discerning intelligence, and clarity of exposition. At the age of 7 Bede entered the monastery of Jarrow in Northumbria and remained there until his death over 50 years later, yet even in this remote corner of Europe he had access to an impressive range of Latin literature, which included Ambrose, Augustine, Jerome, and Gregory the Great. Moreover, he read classical authors, including the complete works of Virgil. His personal copy of a Greek text of the Acts of the Apostles shows that his acquaintance with biblical languages went beyond Latin, because he used it to correct someone else's errors in translation. "I have applied all my diligence to the study of the Scriptures," he summarized shortly before his death, "and observing the regular discipline and keeping the daily service of singing in the church, I have taken delight always either to learn, or to teach, or to write."[2]

Yet it is not Bede's diligent "study of the Scriptures" that has become the cornerstone of his later reputation, but his *Ecclesiastical History*, which may well have been the work best known to Dante. The irony here (if there is any) is that a book with an ostensibly parochial focus – the history of the church in England up to the eighth century – should be prized elsewhere in Europe for so many centuries. While the *History* is not purely theological in the events it narrates, it is nonetheless Christian in tracing the growth of the church in England and in using *exempla* to show God's intervention throughout history. Bede drew from a variety of written and oral sources, but the overall conception of the work is his own, executed in highly polished Latin prose. Indeed for hundreds of years nothing else like it was written in England, until the twelfth and thirteenth centuries when historians like William of Malmesbury began writing synthetic histories once more. And when they did they turned to Bede's *Ecclesiastical History* as a primary source. One tangible measure of its influence is that copies of his *History* survive in about 130 manuscripts throughout England and the rest of Europe.

For many centuries before and after Bede learning and literacy were inseparable from the study of Latin, and with few exceptions the best opportunity for learning Latin was during one's novitiate in religious orders. Thus virtually every man or woman who could read and write was in religious orders, from the dozens of anonymous authors to scholars with an international reputation like Bede and his intellectual heir Alcuin (d. 804), who was the guiding light in the court school of Charlemagne. About 1,000 manuscripts containing Latin survive from Anglo-Saxon England, and no one knows how many have been lost in the intervening centuries, but even this number gives an idea of the relative prestige of Latin in comparison with the more limited number of Old English texts.

In the last decades of the ninth century Bede's *History* was translated into Old English prose, and copies survive in five manuscripts. While obviously competent enough to follow the Latin source word for word, the translator cut about one quarter from the length of Bede's Latin, largely by omitting matters that had been of greater interest to the earlier audience but had lost their appeal, such as the seventh-century dispute over the correct dating of Easter. Almost all of the 51 miracles are retained. Occasionally the translator struggles to find the right Old English construction, but for some of these passages it is difficult to tell whether Bede's demanding syntax is to blame or a corrupt reading in the source manuscript. The passage below, from the story of Cædmon shortly after he confirms his new gift of song, shows two stylistic quirks of the translation. One is the pairing of words in Old English (underscored in the passage below) to translate a single Latin word, perhaps out of a sense that the Latin has connotations that none of the vernacular synonyms quite captures. The other is the use of separate clauses beginning with *ond* to translate some Latinate constructions such as participial phrases and ablative absolutes, which were used more sparingly in Old English:

> Then the abbess began to <u>embrace and love</u> God's gift in the person; and she then <u>exhorted and counseled</u> that he should abandon secular life and take up the monastic life; and he readily consented to it. And she received him into the monastery with his belongings, and added him to the assembly of God's servants, and ordered them to teach him the account of the sacred <u>history and story</u>. And he remembered all that he could learn by hearing, and like a clean cow chewing cud turned it into the sweetest song. And <u>his songs and his poetry</u> were so pleasing to hear that the teachers themselves <u>wrote and learned</u> from his mouth. (*Guide* p. 223, lines 61–70)

The simile of a cow chewing its cud is a deft touch by Bede, which the translator just as deftly carries over into Cædmon's native language. On the one hand it reminds the reader that Cædmon's occupation up to this point has been as a cowherd, so *eodorcende* was an animal behavior he was well familiar with. But Bede's word *ruminando* had an additional set of connotations in the monastic context, where it was a traditional metaphor for the contemplative praxis of "eating" and "digesting" the word of God. "This repeated mastication of the divine words," offers a twentieth-century Benedictine,

> is sometimes described by use of the theme of spiritual nutrition. In this case the vocabulary is borrowed from eating, from digestion, and from the particular form of digestion belonging to ruminants. For this reason,

reading and meditation are sometimes described by the very expressive word *ruminatio*. For example, in praising a monk who prayed constantly Peter the Venerable cried: "Without resting, his mouth ruminated the sacred words."[3]

In today's English the transition of the metaphor from the slow digestion of food to the mental activity of contemplation has been completed, as a glance at a dictionary entry for "ruminate" will show. For Bede, however, the rustic image of a cow chewing cud was a perfect middle term between Cædmon's past life and his new profession as a monk who contemplated divine truths before turning them into poems.

The occasional struggles and small triumphs of the Old English translator remind us that English prose was a relatively underdeveloped mode of writing in comparison with the Latin prose and verse at Bede's disposal. It was also underdeveloped in relation to Old English poetry, which had evolved its own sophisticated style over generations of oral performance. Old English prose needed to generate its own conventions over time, which comes as a surprise to many students today because prose seems intuitively close to the spoken language. But this similarity is largely an illusion, as any transcription of direct speech would show. In the ninth century, when Bede's translator was active, the writing of Old English prose was just beginning to gain some of the conventions it needed, thanks to a new program of education under the patronage of the king of Wessex.

Alfred (871–99) was an unlikely king. Because he was the fifth of five sons of Æthelwulf, king of Wessex, it took an extraordinary set of circumstances to open the throne to him. Barring a palace coup, he could only succeed if the rule passed through each brother in turn and not to any other heir. (In fact the sequence from one brother to the next was more complicated than this summary suggests.) Before the age of 7 Alfred traveled to Rome on two occasions, the second time in the company of his father. Years later Alfred's contemporary biographer Asser tells how the pope received Alfred as an adopted son and anointed him as a future king, but given Alfred's tender age and the fact that his four older brothers were in line for the kingship before him, the interpretation by Asser, whose Latin biography provides much of the basic information we have concerning Alfred despite its eulogistic bias, is a clear case of revisionist history to give Alfred's kingship religious legitimacy. The anointing ceremony might as well have signaled that Alfred's father and the pope were grooming him for a high office in the church.

In 871 the fourth brother died, leaving Wessex to Alfred at a time when the "Great Army" of Vikings had already overtaken much of the kingdom and was poised to conquer it all. Through a series of battles and treaties Alfred checked their advances and began to consolidate his control over Wessex. Eventually he built a system of fortifications, reorganized the national army, instituted a lawcode, and asserted his lordship over much of England. If Alfred's accomplishments ended with his military and political achievements alone he would have been remembered as an outstanding king, but he went further and instituted an unprecedented program of cultural revival. His first concern was to collect a group of scholars from England and abroad to advise him, and among these was his biographer Asser, who joined Alfred's court from his monastery in Wales. Alfred's advisors were a key part of his plan to revive the state of learning in his kingdom, which, he says in a letter addressed to his bishops, had declined to such an alarming level that he was hard pressed to think of clerics who could translate a Latin letter into English.

What was unusual about Alfred's program of revival was the emphasis he gave not only to Latin literacy but to the vernacular as well. In a famous letter addressed to Wærferth, the bishop of Worcester, which forms the preface to his translation of Pope Gregory's *Pastoral Care*, Alfred outlines his plans to promote literacy in conjunction with a project to translate a number of works from Latin into Old English prose. It was such a bold innovation that it may have seemed astonishingly naive to Alfred's contemporaries, given his own lack of scholarly training and the cultural dominance of Latin. His letter seeks to disarm such a reaction by noting how even the word of God was translated into Hebrew, Greek, and Latin because those were the native tongues of the people who received the "law," so it seems reasonable to him to translate scripture and other Latin writings into his own language. They will be available then to a new group of readers, lay and religious, who will be educated in the vernacular:

> Therefore it seems better to me, if it so seems to you, that we should translate into the language that we all can understand certain books that are most necessary for all people to know, and arrange it (as we easily can with God's help if we have peace) that all the youth of free people in

† ÞEOS BOC SCEAL TO WIOGORA CEASTRE

Hatton . 88 .

King Alfred's letter to Bishop Wærferth of Worcester outlining his plan
for education and a program to translate books from Latin into English.
The Bodleian Library, Oxford, Hatton MS 20 folio 1a.

England who have the opportunity to apply themselves should be set to
learning, as long as they are competent for no other employment, until
the time that they can easily read an English document. Afterwards the
training could be advanced to Latin for those whom one wishes to
continue educating and take holy orders. (*Guide* p. 207, lines 54–63)

Alfred's proposal was unusual in promoting literacy in the vernacular first and only afterwards in Latin. For us today the reasonable progression begins with reading and writing our native tongue before applying those skills to a foreign language, but for centuries the standard sequence was always Latin first and foremost, especially when it was part of the training in religious orders (as it nearly always was). Skills for reading and writing the vernacular were added later, if at all. But an important element in Alfred's innovation was to extend the benefits of literacy beyond the ranks of the clerics, which was, again, unusual if not unprecedented for this period. Alfred seems to envision a class of literate secular office-holders who would be able to read royal letters and lawcodes, thus centralizing and extending the king's power.

Alfred's purpose went beyond the practical use of literacy to grease the wheels of his political administration. An important part of his educational program was the systematic translation of "certain books that are most necessary for all people to know" so that their potential readership would include the non-clerical population. The revival of letters under the sponsorship of a king has any number of analogues in medieval history, but a program to teach literacy in the vernacular has far fewer, as does the extended project for translating Latin books. What adds another dimension to the extraordinary ambition of Alfred's plan was his personal involvement as a translator from Latin. It was a demanding task for anyone, especially someone who in his later years complained that he never had the opportunity to learn Latin in his youth. Alfred had to learn it as an adult, somehow, among the various crises he faced as the king of Wessex. It seems likely that the constellation of scholars he called to his court helped him in his translations, but even so a similarity of ideas, phrasings, and idiosyncrasies in translating allows us to identify a body of writing we can with some confidence attribute to Alfred himself. He was, moreover, the prime mover behind a substantial body of ninth-century prose now called Alfredian.

Along with Bede and the other theologians glowing in the sphere of the sun, Beatrice also points out to Dante one, "who exposed the world's deceitfulness to those who hear him rightly." He is a late Roman consul and philosopher named Anicius Manlius Severinus Boethius. Unjustly accused of treason by the Emperor Theodoric, Boethius spent his time in prison writing a short treatise that applies his Christian neo-Platonism to the perennial questions of fate, providence, free will, and the presence of evil in a world created by a good God – questions given more immediacy and poignancy because of his own impending death. He was executed in 524. From the later Middle Ages into the Renaissance *The Consolation of Philosophy* became one of the most widely read works of philosophy, in part because Boethius constructed his arguments by reasoning on purely philosophical grounds without recourse to Christian revelation. The text was also beautifully written, with alternating sections of prose and verse. It has an illustrious history of English translators; after Alfred it was translated by Geoffrey Chaucer and Queen Elizabeth I, among others.

Given its subsequent reception, *The Consolation* may seem like an obvious choice for one of Alfred's "most necessary" books to translate, but it was little known in England at the time. The reasons behind his unusual but prescient choice remain something of a mystery, although his kingdom's struggles with the Viking invaders carry parallels with Boethius' unjust victimization. The Old English text introduces many departures from Boethius' Latin, some of which are explanatory glosses inserted by Alfred, while others were present in the Latin manuscript he worked from. One of the more extensive additions comes at the very beginning, where Alfred gives a brief overview of Boethius and his late antique world, beginning with the conquest of Rome by the Goths. First Theodoric is introduced, and then Boethius: *Þa wæs sum consul, þæt we heretoha hatað, Boetius wæs gehaten, se wæs in boccræftum and on woruldþeawum se rihtwisesta* (*Guide* p. 227, lines 12–14); "There was a certain consul, which we call *here-toha*, named Boethius, who was the most honorable person in scholarship and in worldly customs." An early and crucial change in Alfred's translation is that Boethius was indeed guilty of treason, but he was compelled to plot against Theodoric because the latter was an unjust *cyning* (17–20). This is a daring alteration, because a central presupposition in Boethius' argument is that his unjust accusation becomes an instance of evil in the world, which then becomes the basis for his extended dialogue with Lady Philosophy. One motive for Alfred's change might be his reluctance as a king to admit that royal justice is ever fallible, so if the Roman *cyning* says Boethius is guilty then he must be, but this argument can go only so far, because even in Alfred's version the wickedness of Theodoric motivates and justifies Boethius' rebellion.

Alfred completed the prose translation of *The Consolation of Philosophy*, as he explains in a proem that survives in a twelfth-century manuscript:

Ælfred kuning wæs wealhstod ðisse bec: ond hie of Boclædene on Englisc wende, swa hio nu is gedon. Hwilum he sette word be worde, hwilum angit of andgite, swa swa he hit þa sweotolost ond andgitfullicast gereccan mihte, for þam mistlicum ond manigfealdum weoruldbisgum þe hine oft ægðer ge on mode ge on lichoman bisgodan. (*Anthology* p. 14, lines 1–4)

King Alfred was the translator of this book and rendered it from literary Latin into English, as it is now completed. At times he put it word for word, at times sense for sense just as he could most clearly and intelligently tell it in spite of the various and manifold worldly cares that afflicted him in both mind and body.

Implicit in Alfred's opening lines is an assertion that Old English was capable of accommodating the most sophisticated Latin from late antiquity. Despite its understated formulation, the "word for word" and "sense for sense" statement of procedure carries a bold assumption for a ninth-century vernacular with virtually no literary tradition behind it. Yet Alfred's translation on the whole shows great confidence in the way it deploys the vocabulary and syntax of his language to the task. He adapts the original freely for the relatively unsophisticated readership he has in mind by omitting some of the more opaque passages and inserting explanatory material. Alfred does not hesitate to mention the Christian God or church doctrine, which Boethius consistently kept out. Alfred ends his version of the story of Orpheus and Eurydice, for example, with an overtly Christian allegorization about the need "to flee the darkness of hell and to come to God's true light." It is no longer an account about the pathos of the doomed lovers but a "false story" that nevertheless teaches how each Christian should spurn "his old sins" and not look back on them. The problem with this interpretation is that in turning back to look on *his ealdan yflum* the sinner (Orpheus) loses them, and they return to hell (*Anthology* pp. 16–19).

One of the more fundamental changes is Alfred's decision to replace Boethius with *Mod* ("mind, heart, spirit") and Philosophia with *Wisdom* (or sometimes *Gesceadwisnes*, "intelligence"), which is to replace one kind of abstraction with another. Perhaps Alfred was not sure his audience was familiar with the kind of allegorical personification represented by Philosophia. But the change also had a more practical consequence, because substituting *Mod* for Boethius allows

Alfred to introduce his own voice as a second narrative "I." At times he contributes what can only be considered his own musings on a subject. Thus in a passage on a properly ordered society Alfred sketches out what in later centuries came to be known as the three estates: those who work, those who pray, and those who fight (*Anthology* p. 16, lines 6–13). "Thus I desired the resources to direct my authority," he concludes in an autobiographical vein. "In a word, I wished to live nobly as long as I lived and after my life to leave to the people who came after me my legacy in good works" (p. 16, lines 19–21). This "I" is clearly not the Boethian "I," but Alfred's voice.

The proem goes on to say that Alfred later took the sections corresponding to Latin verse and shaped them into Old English verse, commonly known today as *The Meters of Boethius*. The resulting composite text that alternates between prose and verse mimics the prosimetrum form (alternating sections of prose and verse) of Boethius' original, but modern textual analyses indicate that the versifier was most likely someone other than Alfred. The versification is competent, but from the modern reader's perspective adds little of interest, except for the chance to compare the conventions of Old English verse and prose on an intimate scale.

Among Alfred's other translations that have come down to us are the first 50 Psalms rendered in Old English prose. They are preserved in an eleventh-century manuscript that supplements the first 50 with the remaining Psalms (51–150) in Old English poetry, but these like the versified *Meters of Boethius* were not Alfred's handiwork. He also translated the *Soliloquies* of Augustine of Hippo, which, his preface explains, "concern the reflections and doubts of his mind, how his reason answered his mind when his mind was in doubt about something or wished to know something which previously it had been unable to comprehend clearly."[4] Like *The Consolation of Philosophy* it is an extended dialogue, only this time between St Augustine and Reason, but Alfred adapted Augustine's original far more freely than he did Boethius'. The fourth translation of Alfred known to us is of a book by Gregory the Great which Alfred called *Hierde-boc*, or "Shepherd's book" – shepherding being a common metaphor for the way a bishop or priest should take care of his congregation. Its Latin name is *Regula Pastoralis* or sometimes *Cura Pastoralis*, which gives the name it usually goes by in modern English, *Pastoral Care*. Originally a guide for bishops in administering their dioceses, it contains the kind of practical information that would also be useful in the political administration of his kingdom and thus appealed to Alfred's idea of reform. It was the first text translated by Alfred and apparently circulated to bishops with letters similar to that addressed to Wærferth (above), which outlined the plan for Alfred's education and translation programs. As many have noted, *Pastoral Care* was an inspired choice to inaugurate Alfred's program of cultural revival, not only for the practical information it contained but also because of the particular reverence that the Anglo-Saxons had for Gregory the Great.

Yet another blessed soul seen by Dante among the theologians in the sphere of the sun was Orosius, "that advocate of Christian times" who wrote *Seven Books of History against the Pagans* shortly after the fall of Rome in 410. He compiled it at the urging of Augustine of Hippo, who wanted an authoritative history to oppose the common assumption that Christianity was somehow to blame for the demise of the Roman Empire. The Old English Orosius was not translated by Alfred but emerged from the program of translating the "books most necessary for all people to know." Orosius' *History* was an unsurprising choice because of the useful information it provided about the ancient world, and its typological interpretation of pre-Christian events made it suitable for Christians to read. The anonymous Old English translator freely adapts the Latin original, omitting much and introducing commentary from an impressive range of classical and patristic sources. At the end of an account about the Amazons, for example, "the wretched women" who brutally subjugated much of Europe and Asia, Orosius digresses to the Goths who have conquered Rome, and then generalizes a moral:

> Hu blindlice monege þeoda sprecað ymb þone cristendom, þæt hit nu wyrse sie þonne hit ær wære, þæt hie nellað geþencean oþþe ne cunnon hwær hit gewurde, ær þæm cristendome, þæt ænegu þeod oþre hiere willum friþes bæde, buton hiere þearf wære, oþþe hwær ænegu þeod æt oþerre mehte frið begietan oððe mid golde oððe mid seolfre oþþe mid ænige feo, buton he him underþiedd wære. Ac siþþan Crist geboren wæs, þe ealles middangeardes is sibb and frið, nales þæt an þæt men hie mehten aliesan mid feo of þeowdome, ac eac þeoda him betweonum buton þeowdome gesibbsume wæron. Hu wene ge hwelce sibbe þa weras hæfden ær þæm cristendome, þonne heora wif swa monigfeald yfel donde wæron on þiosan middangearde? (*Reader* p. 26, lines 95–107)

How blindly many people speak about Christianity – that it is now worse than it was before – in that they do not wish to consider or to know how it happened before Christianity that no nation sought peace with another of their own will unless it was necessary, or how no nation could obtain peace from another with gold or silver or with any goods without becoming subjugated to them. But after Christ was born, in whom is friendship and peace for all the earth, not only could people redeem themselves from servitude with goods, but also nations were peaceful among themselves without subjugation. What peace do you expect those men had before Christianity when their women were doing such manifold evil on this earth?

The passage begins with Orosius' general refutation of the charge that things were better before Christianity and ends with a stinging misogynistic allusion to the Amazons, who made life so miserable for the men before Christianity. Orosius implies that things could be worse for his contemporaries: what if women had conquered Rome rather than the manly Goths? The details in the middle of the quoted passage are added by the Old English translator, who spells out the ways one nation can subjugate another and how the coming of Christ changed everything.

One of the more famous interpolations by the translator comes from the first of Orosius' seven books, which describes the geography of the known world. The translator substitutes a more accurate description of the north, followed by what presents itself as a transcription of a first-hand report given by a Norwegian in the service of Alfred: *Ohthere sæde his hlaforde, Ælfrede cyninge, þæt he ealra Norðmonna norþmest bude. He cwæð þæt he bude on þæm lande norþweardum wiþ þa Westsæ* (*Reader* p. 17, lines 1–3); "Ohthere said to his lord King Alfred that of all Norwegians he dwelled the farthest north. He said that he lived in the country northward on the Norwegian Sea." There follows a detailed description of the physical land, its wildlife, and its inhabitants. Ohthere describes a voyage he once took as far north as he could go, eventually turning east around the northern tip of what is now Norway, past what is now Murmansk, Russia, and south into the White Sea. A second traveler named Wulfstan gives a first-hand account (that is, *Wulfstan sæde*) of his journey across the Baltic Sea to the mouth of the Vistula River in what is now Poland. These two interpolations reveal a desire for accuracy in the cultural and physical geography of northern Europe.

The Old English translations of Bede's *Ecclesiastical History of the English People* and Orosius' *History against the Pagans* made available two synthetic histories which between them covered much of the ancient world and more recent English history. Another text that was compiled during Alfred's cultural revival was the *Anglo-Saxon Chronicle*, which recorded events that stretched back before the incarnation of Christ, but its center of gravity falls in eighth-century England and later. To refer to it as a "chronicle" is misleading in an important respect, because it is not a single text (like Bede's *History*) but a composite set of annalistic records that go back to a common "stock," which was compiled during Alfred's reign. Sometime around 892 it was copied and circulated throughout Anglo-Saxon England, where writers in various locations might incorporate material from other written sources as they copied it, and in later years new entries might be transcribed piecemeal or in large blocks. The *Chronicle* was never intended to shape the events under an overarching principle (like a synthetic history). Instead it assembles a year-by-year record of national and sometimes local interest. The information it conveys is often reliable, which makes it the best historical source after Bede for Anglo-Saxon England.

Each folio typically had a running list of the years on the left margin, and for some intervals, for example between the years 200 and 400, there is scarcely an entry. By the end of the ninth century, when the events were contemporary or nearly so, every year has an entry, which can be quite full of details. For a more uneventful year a typical entry might read:

> AN. .dccccxc Her Sigeric wæs gehalgod to arcebisceope, and Eadwine abbod forðferde, and Wulfgar abbod feng to þam rice. (*Guide* p. 213)

> The year 990 In this year Sigeric was consecrated as archbishop [of Canterbury], and Abbot Eadwine passed away, and Wulfgar succeeded to the office of abbot.

The practice of beginning each entry with the Old English word for "Here" derives from the physical location of the entry on the manuscript page immediately next to the roman numeral indicating the year. For other years set pieces apparently composed for some other purpose are inserted as the entries for a given year, such as the dramatic account of the extended feud between Cynewulf and Cyneheard. (See the discussion in chapter 1.) It was entered under the year 757 (incorrectly, it turns out, for 755), when Cynewulf deposed King Sigebriht, but the events narrated under this entry stretch out for 31 years after 755 until Cynewulf dies. A separate entry for 786 notes that "Cyneheard killed King Cynewulf" and that he was later slain "there" (in Merton) along with 84 of his men.

Another instance where the *Chronicle* breaks from its usual terse prose style – in fact it bursts into song – is found among the entries for King Æthelstan's reign. Beginning with the year 931 the following excerpts give a sense of the restrained, matter-of-fact prose, until 937:

931   In this year Byrnstan was consecrated as bishop of Winchester on May 29th, and he held the see for two and a half years.
932   In this year Bishop Frithestan died.
933   In this year King Athelstan traveled to Scotland with an army and a fleet and devastated much of it. And Bishop Byrnstan passed away in Winchester on the feast of All Saints.
934   In this year Bishop Ælfheah succeeded to the episcopal see [of Winchester].
937   In this year

> King Æthelstan,   lord of earls,
> ring-giver of warriors,   and also his brother
> Prince Edmund   won everlasting glory
> in battle around Brunanburh.

(*Anthology* pp. 28–30, lines 3–13)

There follows the complete text of a 73-line poem written out as prose (as is virtually every other copy of Old English poems), so that only on closer inspection can a reader see that the genre has shifted. *The Battle of Brunanburh* is a panegyric that must have been composed within decades after the battle, because the earliest surviving copy dates from around 955. And the only four versions of it comprise *Chronicle* entries. It could have started off as an oral poem that the annalist found and opportunistically recorded as the entry for 937, but some have noticed a bookish and historical quality to the poem in addition to its command of the heroic verse conventions, which raises the possibility that it was composed with the annal entry in mind. In any case the battle commemorated by the poem was of considerable consequence because it eliminated a threat to Æthelstan's hold over Mercia and Wessex, which allowed him and his successors eventually to expand their power over all of England. (For more discussion of *The Battle of Brunanburh* see chapter 1.)

Other entries beginning with the latter part of Alfred's reign are particularly full, not because a set piece from elsewhere has been inserted, but because the prose of the anonymous chronicle writer (or writers) shows an increasing confidence and sophistication in handling the genre. The entry for 892, for example, is full of details that make sense only in the larger context created by the equally full entries before and after it, so that the writer, assuming the voice of a narrating "we," can make references to other passages *þe we gefyrn ymbe spræcon* ("which we spoke about before"), as in the first sentence below:

892   In this year the great [Viking] army, which we spoke about before, went back from the eastern kingdom westward to *Bunnan* [Boulogne], and there they were provided with ships so that they crossed over with horses and everything on a single journey; and they came up into the mouth of the Lympne River with two hundred and fifty ships. The mouth is in the eastern part of Kent at the east end of the great forest we call *Andred*. From east to west the forest is 120 miles long or longer, and thirty miles wide. The river that we spoke of earlier flows out of the *Weald* [= the great forest]. They rowed their ships up to the *Weald* four miles away from the mouth. And there they stormed a fortress in the fen; only a few free peasants occupied it and it was half-built.

Then immediately afterwards *Hæsten* with eighty ships came up to the mouth of the Thames, and built a great fortification at Milton and the army made one at Appledore. (*Reader* pp. 34–5, lines 1–15)

One of the remarkable things about this entry is what *does not* happen. No prominent official dies; no battle takes place; no bishop takes up his office. Instead the reader is given a detailed account of the movements of two Viking armies, one of which engages in a skirmish, but no more. It is full of details of location, the direction of movement, numbers and measurements, and the names of rivers and other geographical features. They constitute precisely the kind of information needed to reconstruct the events after the fact, and indeed it has allowed modern historians to map out the movements of the armies in question.⁵ The richness of these details contributes to a more comprehensive account of Alfred's last battles against the Viking armies threatening Wessex in the early years of his reign, and they were written shortly afterwards while the battles were still in living memory.

The year 892 was significant in another way for the *Anglo-Saxon Chronicle*. It was the year when copies of it were first circulated to other sites around England. The wider appeal of the *Chronicle* is apparent from the way different versions of it were updated for long periods after 892, some of them even after the Norman Conquest. One of these, from Peterborough Abbey (in the East Midlands), continues its entries up to 1154.

When English prose reached a level of competence and maturity after the sponsorship of Alfred's program for translating the "most necessary" books, it became adaptable to other kinds of writings. *Apollonius of Tyre* is a prose translation of uncertain date that closely follows its Latin source, *Historia Apollonii Regis Tyri*. It is something of an anomaly in that it provides a fully developed secular romance centuries before Arthurian romances began to circulate. Yet it displays many of the hallmarks of the later genre as its protagonist survives plots against his life, shipwreck, exile, mistaken identity, and the frustrations of love. The plot is episodic, driven by the random twists of fate known in later centuries as *aventure*, yet throughout all his trials Apollonius' innate nobility reveals itself. For example, after a shipwreck he washes up naked near Pentapolis in *Ciriniscan lande* ("the country of Cyrenaica"), where a herald announces that the king will hold games in the city's *bæð-stede* ("bath-place" or "gymnasium"). Because the participants compete in the nude, Apollonius' own nakedness is no longer an issue, and he comes to the king's attention after he outperforms everyone else. The king clothes him and invites him to his court, where after a royal feast (*cynelic gebeorscipe*) he performs so beautifully on the harp that he becomes like Apollo, "the god of heathens" (*ðara hæðenra god*). The king's daughter notices him and "then her heart fell in love with him" (*þa gefeol hyre mod on his lufe*) (*Anthology* pp. 242–6). A happy marriage cannot be far off.

In later centuries *Historia Apollonii* was destined to become a perennial favorite, and it even supplies the plot for Shakespeare's *Pericles*, but in light of the usual content and contexts of Old English prose, it is hard to place a tale of adventure that begins with a father's unpunished incest against his own daughter and includes pagan priestesses and brothels within its imaginary landscape. Like the other translations discussed in this chapter it reveals a scholar's command of Latin and a developed prose style. But why was it translated and preserved? Who read it? Despite its pagan content, was it read as though it provided moral lessons for a Christian audience? The only surviving copy of *Apollonius* forms part of an eleventh-century manuscript collection, where it makes a strange bedfellow for dozens of legal and religious pieces. A few folios after it ends, for example, there is an Old English translation of part of Genesis and paraphrases of the Lord's Prayer and the Gloria in alliterative verse.

Apollonius, the narrative tells us, "trusted in his intelligence and in scholarly learning" (*getruwode on his snotornesse and on ða boclican lare*, *Anthology* p. 236, line 37). When he hears that King Antiochus of Antioch will give his beautiful daughter in marriage to the first suitor who can answer a riddle, he decides to take up the challenge. The king's *rædels* is self-incriminating, as Apollonius will soon discover. Antiochus delivers it in two parts:

> "*Scelere vereor, materna carne vescor.*" It is in English: "I suffer wickedness, I enjoy the mother's flesh." Next he said: "*Quaero patrem meum, meae matris virum, uxoris meae filiam nec invenio.*" It is in English: "I seek my father, my mother's husband, my wife's daughter, and I may not find them." After Apollonius truly heard the riddle, he turned aside slightly from the king, and when he considered it in his mind, he solved it with wisdom, and he discerned the truth with God's help. He turned back to the king and said, "Good King, you set the riddle, hear the explanation. When you said that you suffer wickedness, you are not lying about that. Look at yourself. And when you said 'I enjoy the mother's flesh,' you are not lying about that. Look at your daughter." (*Anthology* p. 236, lines 44–52)

The correct answer is the father's incest with his daughter, as Apollonius figures out because of his *wisdom*. His wisdom also tells him, however, that he and any other suitor shrewd enough to perceive his crime will be murdered by Antiochus, which will also indefinitely postpone the day that he must give his daughter in marriage. Apollonius immediately flees back to Tyre, but Antiochus' murderers follow him, so he sails away and into more adventures.

Apollonius needs to solve only the first riddle to know the crime, and he does not even mention the second. The key is identifying who or what can occupy the subject position, the "I" who suffers and enjoys. The surprising twist is that the right answer is the least obvious candidate, Antiochus himself, because riddles that ask to identify the "I" conventionally make the answer anyone or anything *but* the person actually speaking. Also complicating Apollonius' task are the connotations of some key words in the Latin; for example, besides meaning "to enjoy" generally, *vescor* also means "to eat," which would then change the interpretation of *carne* to a different kind of flesh. Because the double meaning of *vescor* is unavailable, the Old English translator supplies another doublet with *scylde*, which means either "crime" or "guilt," but either of these is perfectly suited to Antiochus. In the second riddle the speaking "I" is the daughter herself, who cannot find her father or herself (her mother's daughter) because Antiochus is now her *vir* and she is now his *uxor*.

Despite the exotic setting and conventions of the *Historia Apollonii*, the Old English translator was working with a familiar genre in adapting the Latin riddle into the vernacular. Over 90 Old English riddles have been written down in the Exeter Book, which cover a wide range of riddling types, from pious meditations on the mysteries of all creation to witty personifications of a bellows. Some are more cerebral, with bookish pedigrees drawn from compositions by Latin scholars, while others are from humbler backgrounds. There is even one that (as in *Apollonius*) explores the entangled lines of kinship after an incestuous relationship:

> Wær sæt æt wine   mid his wifum twam
> ond his twegen suno   ond his twa dohtor,
> swase gesweostor   ond hyra suno twegen,
> freolico frumbearn;   fæder wæs þær inne
> þara æþelinga,   æghwæðres mid
> eam ond nefa.   Ealra wæron fife
> eorla ond idesa   insittendra.
>
> (*Anthology* p. 72, Riddle 46)

A man sat at wine with his two wives and his two sons and his two daughters, dear sisters, and their two noble firstborn sons; the father of each of the princes was there, uncle and nephew. In all there were five men and women sitting inside.

A headcount of all the relatives mentioned gives a (conservative) tally of eleven; yet the final line says there were only five. How can this be? The answer is to be found in the book of Genesis: Lot's two daughters slept with him after making him drunk, and each had a son by him. (The clerics who preserved the riddle must have appreciated this bit of levity lifted from sacred scripture.) In fact the riddle is sparing in its enumeration of Lot's convoluted web of relationships. Try to follow the lines from just one node in the family tree: each son is brother, cousin, and uncle to the other; each is the brother of his mother and is the brother, cousin, brother-in-law, and grandson of his mother's sister; each is the son, grandson, nephew, and brother-in-law of Lot. Each may also be a grandnephew of Lot, depending on how the lines are drawn. Is it any wonder that incest is an almost universal human taboo?

Both "Lot and his Daughters" and the two riddles in *Apollonius* are fairly simple conundrums where the words actually conceal very little. Each of Lot's sons *is* the uncle and nephew to the other. The solution depends upon seeing one key (incest) that makes the apparent paradox fall away. Most riddles, however, use various tricks of language to conceal the solution even as they elaborate it. Riddles typically fall into two main groups. In one the object speaks with its own voice, using the rhetorical device of prosopopoeia as with the talking cross in *The Dream of the Rood*. (See the discussion in chapter 3.) For example, Riddle 85 from the Exeter Book reads:

> Nis min sele swige,   ne ic sylfa hlud
> ymb dryhtsele;   unc dryhten scop
> siþ ætsomne.   Ic eom swiftra þonne he,
> þragum strengra,   he þreohtigra.
> Hwilum ic me reste;   he sceal rinnan forð.
> Ic him in wunige   a þenden ic lifge;
> gif wit unc gedælað,   me bið dead witod.
>
> (*Guide* p. 234)

> My hall is not silent, nor am I loud around the splendid hall; the Lord created the two of us for a journey together. I am swifter than he, at times stronger; he is more enduring. At times I rest; he must run forth. I will dwell in him for as long as I live; if we two are separated, death will be appointed for me.

The "I" speaks for itself and its close companion, who seems to have human traits but is also a hall; yet it could not be a real hall because it must move constantly. And the "I" may never leave it. The identity of the speaking "I" is a fish, whose "hall" is the water. Despite its humble topic, this one derives from a Latin riddle, "Flumen et Piscis" by Symphosius, a late classical author who compiled a collection of 100 three-line riddles. But the Old English version expands on the Latin in significant ways.

Once the answer is pointed out the reader can return to the clues and reconstruct how they lead to the solution. In this case, as with many riddles, the objects adopt human traits: the fish, of course, speaks like a hall-dwelling person. But there is a difference, which is the first clue: the riddle's hall makes noise and the inhabitant is silent, which is the exact opposite of the human side of things. The hall is also capable of motion, especially running (*rinnan*), a word which then as now could apply to both water and humans. Even the riddle's pronouns maintain the double focus on object and human, because in the grammatical gender system of Old English a masculine noun like *sele* takes the pronoun *he*, and *he* is then maintained throughout the riddle, where it suggests "man" without sacrificing its antecedent *sele*. The natural gender system of Modern English, by contrast, allows only "it" for most non-humans (some animals also merit "he" or "she," but not many), so using "he" in a fish riddle today would overplay the personification.

The other kind of riddle is where an object is described, either as a simple third person account, "X is," or one that begins "I saw X," like Riddle 51:

> Ic seah wrætlice   wuhte feower
> samed siþian;   swearte wæran lastas
> swaþu swiþe blacu.   Swift wæs on fore,
> fuglum framra;   fleag on lyfte,
> deaf under yþe.   Dreag unstille
> winnende wiga   se him wegas tæcneþ
> ofer fæted gold   feower eallum.
>
> (*Guide* p. 238)

I saw four marvelous creatures travelling together; their footprints were dark, very black tracks. It was swift on the journey, stronger than birds;

it flew in the air, dove under the wave. Restlessly the struggling warrior persevered who directed the paths for all four of them over the ornamented gold.

This is one of several riddles that smell of the scriptorium. The four "creatures" are a quill pen held by a thumb and two fingers. The ink leaves behind dark "tracks," and when the pen darts back and forth to the inkwell it "flies" faster than birds – it is even feathered for flight. There is a subtle "in joke" in this riddle, which characterizes a monastic scribe as a "struggling warrior" (*winnende wiga*), when the truth is probably closer to Samuel Johnson's self-definition of a lexicographer as "a harmless drudge." It is not a case of applying human traits to something else, but rather taking the poetic register usually reserved for those who fight and applying it to those who pray. And in this heroic context the *fæted gold* calls to mind the splendid gold treasures and armaments in a hall like Heorot before the riddle's solution flattens it to gold leaf on a manuscript folio.

It is a common convention for riddles to cloak non-human creatures in anthropomorphism, but Old English can take the disguise to a second level by applying the specialized vocabulary drawn from heroic poetry. The more unlikely the *wiht* for the heroic register, the more entertaining the results, as with Riddle 29:

> Ic wiht geseah   wundorlice
> hornum bitweonum   huþe lædan,
> lyftfæt leohtlic,   listum gegierwed,
> huþe to þam ham   of þam heresiþe:
> walde hyre on þære byrig   bur atimbran,
> searwum asettan,   gif hit swa meahte.
> Ða cwom wundorlicu wiht   ofer wealles hrof –
> seo is eallum cuð   eorðbuendum –
> ahredde þa þa huþe,   ond to ham bedraf
> wreccan ofer willan;   gewat hyre west þonan
> fæhþum feran;   forð onette.
> Dust stonc to heofonum,   deaw feol on eorþan,
> niht forð gewat.   Nænig siþþan
> wera gewiste   þære wihte sið.

(*Anthology*, p. 70)

I saw a creature amazingly carrying booty between horns, a bright air-vessel skillfully adorned, [carrying] booty home from the war-expedition:

she wished to build a cottage in the city, to set it up cunningly, if she could do it so. When a remarkable creature came over the wall's roof – he is known to all earth's inhabitants – he recaptured the booty and drove the fugitive home unwillingly; she went travelling west from the feud there; she hastened away. Dust rose to the heavens, dew fell on the earth, night went forth. Afterwards no man knew the creature's journey.

The heroic tone is set by the three-fold repetition of *huþe*, which as "booty" is more common in poems with a martial context, as for example with Grendel, the "evil *wiht*" who takes his grisly booty of 30 Danish warriors to his home "exulting in booty" (*Wiht unhælo . . . huþe hremig to ham faran, Beowulf* lines 120, 124). Other word choices contribute to the martial context, such as "war-expedition," "fugitive," and "feud." Even the description of the booty as cunningly contrived echoes the kinds of treasure that legendary Germanic warriors would bring back from a successful battle. The two *wihte* in the riddle's solution are the moon and sun, which are about as far removed from the heroic ethos as anything can be, yet the anthropomorphism is cleverly sustained. The Anglo-Saxons knew that the moon's light was reflected from the sun. Thus the moon is a plundering warrior who steals the sun's light but is later forced to give it back. The *lyft-fæt leohtlic* or "bright air-vessel" is light itself, which the moon has taken from the sun and carries "between horns." When it is new the "horned" moon appears as a thin crescent with the shaded part barely visible between its horns. It rises just before dawn to begin its westward journey across the sky, but before long the sun appears and "recaptures" its light as night goes away.

Most riddles, however, do not depend on specialized lore for their solutions. A subset of the Exeter Book riddles take delight in spelling out their obvious double entendres:

> Wrætlic hongað   bi weres þeo,
> frean under sceate.   Foran is þyrel,
> bið stiþ ond heard,   stede hafað godne.
> Þonne se esne   his agen hrægl
> ofer cneo hefeð,   wile þæt cuþe hol
> mid his hangellan   heafde gretan
> þæt he efenlang ær   oft gefylde.
> (*Anthology* p. 72, Riddle 44)

A marvel hangs by a man's thigh, under a lord's cloak. A hole is in front, it is stiff and hard, it has a good position. When the man hoists his own garment over his knee, he wishes to visit with his hanging thing the well-known hole, which he had often filled to the entire length.

The first lines pointedly refrain from using pronouns, where the gender might give away too much. *Wrætlic* as an adjective is ambiguous in gender, but it supplies the subject of *hongað* and two of the next three verbs. The "real" answer is a key, which hangs by a cord on a man's belt and is used in *þæt cuþe hol,* or the keyhole that is "well-known" because the key is designed to fit snugly inside the entire length of the lock. The "real" answer is supposed to rescue the squeamish reader from any discomfort with the obvious phallic meaning, but of course "penis" is just as legitimate a solution, if not more so, because it is the first one that comes to mind. If it did not the joke would be lost.

The double entendre riddles raise interesting questions of interpretation because the genre conventionally calls for one and only one solution. When we say "I get it" in response to "What does it mean?," the response is just an expression of convenience prompted by the game, which asks us to wrap up all the clues in one solution. The correct answer is often equated with the riddle's "meaning," which is also implied when we say "I get it" – as if meaning in its entirety can disclose itself to our comprehension. This way of thinking about the solution points to a deeper lesson about the way riddles manipulate meaning. "What they mean," summarizes Craig Williamson,

> is that reality exists and is at the same time a mosaic of man's perception. What they mean is that man's measure of the world is in words, that perceptual categories are built on verbal foundations, and that by withholding the key to the categorical house (the entitling solution) the riddlers may force the riddle-solver to restructure his own perceptual blocks in order to gain entry to a metaphorical truth. In short the solver must imagine himself a door and open in.[6]

None of the Old English riddles from the Exeter Book comes with a solution provided in the manuscript, so most of the solutions given in discussions like this one depend on a loose consensus by modern scholars, who like Apollonius of Tyre bring all kinds of ingenuity and *boclic lar* to the task. But some solutions are still in dispute or unknown. For still others there is little doubt because they derive from Latin riddles by Symphosius and other scholars. They give away the solution in titles like "Flumen et Piscis" ("River and Fish"), which leave no suspense for the reader. Oddly enough, whether the solution is an educated guess by modern scholars, or whether it is affirmed by a Latin source, the mental exercise of puzzling out the way a riddle works brings the reader to consider the relation between language and our experience of the world.

Starting with a simple idea or object, a riddle meditates on its nature from an off-center point of view, but throughout this mental exercise it must refrain from *naming* it. Naming is, of course, the most efficient way to identify something, but the efficiency comes at the cost of foreclosing further thinking about it. A riddle induces the reader to follow its imaginative musings down unfamiliar paths as it circles around a mystery that eventually turns out to be something that is intimately familiar, after all. When a riddle forces us to consider the moon as a plundering warrior, for example, it disrupts our usual categories of thought for the moon and for warriors, but in puzzling through the momentary confusion of one with the other, we come to see that our usual ways of perceiving reality are arbitrary conventions. Why *do* we think of the moon through one set of terms and not another? To ask the question opens up a new universe of possibilities.

The riddles also remind their readers how much our perception of reality depends on verbal constructions, but they do so by playful misdirection. If language is inherently metaphorical, riddles take the allusiveness of the trope to a higher level. A conventional metaphor might say "the moon plunders the light of the sun." But what happens when we remove the identities of "moon" and "sun" from the formulation? The names no longer anchor the metaphoric play, so the trope is set adrift on its own imaginative currents – and we gain a riddle of the moon and the sun. So in the end riddles do not reduce meaning to a single solution as much as they reveal how language represents reality. In their own way, riddles invite an exercise of close reading familiar to literary students today, who tease out the polysemy and indeterminacy of meaning that characterize all kinds of imaginative literature.

Near the end of the tenth century Ælfric took stock of the current state of learning in England, which he found in much better condition than King Alfred did a century earlier in his letter to Bishop Wærferth. The monastic revival begun by Dunstan and Athelwold in the decades after 950 had produced a new flowering of scholarship, especially in monasteries. While its main focus was on religion, an important byproduct of the revival was the copying of manuscripts containing the major Old English literary texts that survive today, including the *Beowulf* manuscript, the Exeter Book, the Vercelli Book, and of course the religious prose of Ælfric and his contemporaries. Ælfric's survey of the current state of learning forms part of the Old English Preface to his grammar of Latin, which he wrote in Old English for "young children at the beginning of the skill [*cræft*] until they arrived at greater understanding" (*Ælfric* p. 115, lines 4–5). His decision to produce an introductory textbook immediately after his two great series of *Catholic Homilies* was motivated by a sense of responsibility for the future health of monastic learning. The fate of his *Grammar* (or *Stæf-cræft*) vindicated his decision because it survives in over a dozen manuscripts and continued to be used well after the Norman Conquest. The next English grammar of Latin was not produced until the fourteenth century.

Ælfric supplemented his *Grammar* with two other introductory pedagogic works, a *Glossary* and a *Colloquy* consisting of lively dialogues in simple Latin that the budding scholars memorized for delivery during their lessons. (An Old English version of the same dialogue was "back engineered" by Henry Sweet in 1897. He took the glosses that Anglo-Saxon students once scribbled between the lines of Ælfric's Latin *Colloquy* and recast them as Old English sentences for today's students to translate into Modern English. See *Guide* pages 182–9.) From the preface to Ælfric's *Grammar*, however, it is clear that the general state of learning in England was already at an advanced level, and his concern was that it be maintained:

> It is fitting for young people that they learn some wisdom, and it is fitting for their elders that they teach some discernment to their youth, because the faith will be maintained by doctrine, and each person who loves wisdom will be happy. And whoever wishes neither to learn nor to teach, if he can, then his understanding will grow cold to sacred doctrine and he will move little by little from God. Where shall wise teachers for God's people come from unless they learn in their youth? And how can the faith be advanced if the doctrine and the teachers fall away? It is necessary now to warn zealously God's servants and monks so that the holy doctrine will not grow cold or fall away in our days as it had done among the English a few years ago, such that no English

priest knew how to compose or understand a letter in Latin, until Archbishop Dunstan and Bishop Athelwold re-established teaching in the monastic life. (*Ælfric* pp. 115–16, lines 10–23)

The allusion to the desperate state in earlier years is a direct reference to Alfred's letter to Wærferth, which claims that he knew of no priest south of the Humber River who could translate a letter (*ærendgewrit*) from Latin to English (*Guide* p. 205, line 16). Whether or not the situation was as dire as Alfred claimed, Ælfric can take some comfort in contrasting the level of scholarship that his mentors Dunstan and Athelwold re-established (*eft . . . arærde*) in his own days. At the same time the state of learning in the ninth century served as a warning against complacency – hence the emphasis on the responsibility that should motivate teachers and their students.

It is interesting that both Alfred's program of education and Ælfric's pedagogic writings should emphasize (sensibly enough) the importance of teaching the young, but Alfred directed his attention to literacy in the vernacular, while Ælfric was concerned with Latin because of its crucial importance in the monasteries. Yet the flowering of so much scholarship in both Latin and Old English during Ælfric's lifetime owes a great deal to the program of education established a century earlier, although King Alfred could not have guessed the direction that scholarship would take.

Notes

INTRODUCTION

1   The classic work on medieval figural interpretation is *"Figura,"* by Erich Auerbach in his *Scenes from the Drama of European Literature* (New York: Meridian, 1959), pp. 11–76. The quotation is from Michel Foucault, *The Archaeology of Knowledge and the Discourse on Language*, trans. A. M. Sheridan Smith (New York: Pantheon, 1972), p. 129.

CHAPTER 1 THE VOW

1   Patrick Wormald, *The Making of English Law: King Alfred to the Twelfth Century*, vol. 1 (Oxford: Blackwell, 1999), p. 143.

2   Leofflæd, however, owned land elsewhere. See Pauline Stafford, "Women and the Norman Conquest," *Transactions of the Royal Historical Society*, 6th series, IV (1994): 221–49 at 242–3.

3   See the discussion on the various meanings of *getrywða* and similar words in the first chapter of R. F. Green, *A Crisis of Truth: Literature and Law in Ricardian England* (Philadelphia: University of Pennsylvania Press, 1999).

4   Ælfric quotes the Latin Vulgate in the last line: *Perdes omnes qui loquuntur mendacium* (Psalm 5:7). This and all subsequent English quotations from the Bible come from the Douai-Rheims translation of the Latin Vulgate: Holy Bible (Baltimore, MD: John Murphy, 1914). Ælfric, *Wyrdwriteras*, is quoted from John C. Pope, ed., *Homilies of Ælfric: A Supplementary Collection*, 2 vols (London: Oxford University Press, 1967–8), vol. 2, pp. 731–2, lines 95–103.

5   *Njal's Saga*, chapter 34. Quoted from the translation by Robert Cook (London: Penguin, 2001).

6   Tacitus, *Germania*, trans. J. B. Rives, Clarendon Ancient History Series (Oxford: Clarendon Press, 1999), para. 14.1.
7   James Campbell et al., eds, *The Anglo-Saxons* (Oxford: Phaidon, 1982), p. 193.
8   Antonette DiPaolo Healey et al., eds, *The Dictionary of Old English* (Toronto: Pontifical Institute for Mediaeval Studies, 1986–), is in the midst of its project to publish fascicles for each letter of the alphabet.
9   For a perceptive study of this rhetorical exchange, see Fred C. Robinson, "God, Death, and Loyalty in *The Battle of Maldon*," in *J. R. R. Tolkien, Scholar and Storyteller: Essays in Memoriam*, eds Mary Salu and Robert T. Farrell (Ithaca, NY: Cornell University Press, 1979), pp. 76–98.
10 See Daniel Donoghue, ed., and Seamus Heaney, trans. *Beowulf: A Verse Translation* (New York: Norton, 2002), pp. xxiii–xxxviii.
11 See Laurence DeLooze, "Frame Narratives and Fictionalization: Beowulf as Narrator," *Texas Studies in Literature and Language* 26 (1984): 145–56; reprinted in R. D. Fulk, ed., *Interpretations of "Beowulf": A Critical Anthology* (Bloomington: Indiana University Press, 1991), pp. 242–50.

CHAPTER 2 THE HALL

1   See Leslie Webster, "Archaeology and *Beowulf*," in *Beowulf*, pp. 183–94; reprinted in Daniel Donoghue, ed., and Seamus Heaney, trans. *Beowulf: A Verse Translation*, (New York: Norton, 2002), pp. 212–36; Rosemary Cramp, "The Hall in *Beowulf* and in Archaeology," in Helen Damico and John Leyerle, eds, *Heroic Poetry in the Anglo-Saxon Period: Studies in Honor of Jess B. Bessinger, Jr.* (Kalamazoo: Medieval Institute Publications, 1993), pp. 331–46.
2   *Njal's Saga*, trans. Robert Cook (London: Penguin, 2001). The manuscript's Icelandic title is *Brennu-Njals Saga* or *The Saga of the Burning of Njal*.
3   In more recent centuries the Book of Judith has been considered apocryphal by Protestant denominations; Roman Catholics call it deuterocanonical (meaning "a second canon" added later).
4   After the ninth Psalm, the Latin Vulgate numbering is off by one in comparison with later Bibles (and the Hebrew), because the Vulgate combines two separate psalms within number 9. Thus, for example, the Vulgate's Psalm 113 is number 114 elsewhere.
5   The "Letter to Can Grande" is Epistola X in *Dantis Alagherii Epistolae: The Letters of Dante*, ed. Paget Toynbee (Oxford: Clarendon Press, 1920). See also Eric Auerbach, "*Figura*," *Scenes from the Drama of European Literature* (New York: Meridian, 1959), pp. 53–4.
6   See Allen Frantzen, *Before the Closet: Same-Sex Love from Beowulf to Angels in America* (Chicago: University of Chicago Press, 1998), pp. 68–107. For

later centuries see C. Stephen Jaeger, *Ennobling Love: In Search of a Lost Sensibility* (Philadelphia: University of Pennsylvania Press, 1999), *passim*.

7   See Malcolm Godden, "Anglo-Saxons on the Mind," in Michael Lapidge and Helmut Gneuss, eds, *Learning and Literature in Anglo-Saxon England: Studies Presented to Peter Clemoes* (Cambridge: Cambridge University Press, 1985) for the various shades of meaning for words like *sefa, hyge, mod,* all of which can mean some combination of mind, heart, memory, spirit, thought, emotion. Most significantly, the Anglo-Saxons did not insist on a clean distinction between thoughts and feelings, which in Western society is a legacy of Greek philosophy and more recently Descartes.

8   Quoted from Donald A. Bullough, "What Has Ingeld to Do with Lindisfarne?," *Anglo-Saxon England* 22 (1993): 93–125, at 124.

CHAPTER 3 THE MIRACLE

1   Bede, *Historical Works*, trans. J. E. King, Loeb Classical Library, 2 vols (Cambridge, MA: Harvard University Press, 1976), book iv, ch. 23.

2   See Michael Lapidge, "The Saintly Life in Anglo-Saxon England," in Malcolm Godden and Michael Lapidge, eds, *The Cambridge Companion to Old English Literature* (Cambridge: Cambridge University Press, 1991), pp. 243–63.

3   The standard edition for the *Guthlac* poems is G. P. Krapp and E. V. K. Dobbie, eds, *The Exeter Book*, Anglo-Saxon Poetic Records 3 (New York: Columbia University Press, 1936).

4   *Juliana* is edited in Krapp and Dobbie, *Exeter Book. Andreas* is in G. P. Krapp, ed., *The Vercelli Book*, Anglo-Saxon Poetic Records 2 (New York: Columbia University Press, 1932).

5   Translation by Jonathan Wilcox in *Ælfric* p. 131; Latin on pp. 119–20. On the sources and arrangement of the *Lives* see *Ælfric* pp. 45–51. The exact shape of Ælfric's *Lives of Saints* has been complicated by a number of non-Ælfrician items included in the most complete manuscript.

6   On the anonymous saints' lives see D. G. Scragg and Elaine Treharne, "The Corpus of Anonymous Lives and their Manuscript Context," in *Holy Men and Holy Women: Old English Prose Saints' Lives and Their Context*, ed. Paul E. Szarmach (Albany, NY: State University of New York Press, 1996), pp. 209–25. On the cult of Mary see the edition of three apocryphal gospels by Mary Clayton, *The Apocryphal Gospels of Mary in Anglo-Saxon England*, Cambridge Studies in Anglo-Saxon England 26 (Cambridge: Cambridge University Press, 1998).

7   See for example A. C. Spearing, *Medieval Dream Poetry* (Cambridge: Cambridge University Press, 1976).

8   W. J. T. Mitchell, *Picture Theory: Essays on Verbal and Visual Representation* (Chicago: University of Chicago Press, 1994), p. 152.
9   Kevin Crossley-Holland, trans., *The Exeter Riddle Book* (London: Folio Society, 1978), p. 55.
10 Crossley-Holland, *Exeter Riddle Book*, p. 51.
11 See the collection edited by Brendan Cassidy, *The Ruthwell Cross* (Princeton, NJ: Princeton University Press, 1992). For the date of the cross see Richard N. Bailey, *England's Earliest Sculptors*, Publications of the Dictionary of Old English 5 (Toronto: Pontifical Institute of Mediaeval Studies, 1996), pp. 43–5.
12 For a photographic reproduction see David Wilson, *Anglo-Saxon Art from the Seventh Century to the Norman Conquest* (Woodstock, NY: Overlook Press, 1984), p. 191.

CHAPTER 4 THE PULPIT

1   Dorothy Whitelock, "The Interpretation of *The Seafarer*," in Cyril Fox and B. Dickins, eds, *The Early Cultures of North West Europe* (*H. M. Chadwick Memorial Studies*) (Cambridge: Cambridge University Press, 1950), pp. 261–72. The irony of Whitelock's influence on the reception of the poem is that she was the most recent editor of *Reader* when, in 1967, she saw fit to continue printing the poem without its final 16 lines. On the motivations of early generations of scholars see Allen J. Frantzen, *Desire for Origins: New Language, Old English, and Teaching the Tradition* (New Brunswick, NJ: Rutgers University Press, 1990).
2   John C. Pope, ed., *The Homilies of Ælfric: A Supplementary Collection*, 2 vols (Oxford: Oxford University Press, 1967–8), glossary entry for *uton*.
3   See D. G. Scragg, "The Corpus of Vernacular Homilies and Prose Saints' Lives before Ælfric," *Anglo-Saxon England* 8 (1979): 223–77.
4   From Ælfric's Latin introduction, *simplicem Anglicam*: see *Ælfric* p. 107, translation p. 127. The introduction also emphasizes the need for orthodoxy and points out that the collection includes not just homilies expounding the gospel but also saints' lives.
5   The homily's formal closing is followed by an explanation of the meaning of Septuagesima Sunday. For the text see Malcolm Godden, ed., *Ælfric's Catholic Homilies* (London: Oxford University Press, 1979), pp. 49–51.
6   R. Morris, ed., *The Blickling Homilies of the Tenth Century* (London: Oxford University Press, 1880; reprint 1967), pp. 117, 119.
7   See M. Godden, "Apocalypse and Invasion in Late Anglo-Saxon England," in Malcolm Godden, Douglas Gray, and Terry Hoad, eds, *From Anglo-Saxon to Early Middle English: Studies Presented to E. G. Stanley* (Oxford:

Clarendon Press, 1994), p. 132. The passage from Ælfric's homily is quoted from P. A. M. Clemoes, ed., *Ælfric's Catholic Homiles: The First Series Text* (Oxford: Oxford University Press, 1997), p. 347, lines 60–1.

8   Milton McC. Gatch, *Preaching and Theology in Anglo-Saxon England: Ælfric and Wulfstan* (Toronto: University of Toronto Press, 1977), p. 80.

9   The quotation from Gregory's *Morals on Job 7.45* is taken from Bernard McGinn, "The Last Judgment in Christian Tradition," in Bernard McGinn, ed., *The Encyclopedia of Apocalypticism*, vol. 2 (New York: Continuum, 1998), p. 379. The letter to Æthelbert is preserved in Bede's *Ecclesiastical History*, book 1, chapter 32.

10   Gatch, *Preaching and Theology*, p. 105.

11   Patrick Wormald, *The Making of English Law: King Alfred to the Twelfth Century*, Vol. 1, 2 vols (Oxford: Blackwell, 1999), p. 450.

CHAPTER 5 THE SCHOLAR

1   The Latin title translates as "Ecclesiastical History of the English People." Elsewhere Bede rephrased the latter half of the title: ". . . of the British and most of all (*maxime*) the English People" and ". . . of our island and people."

2   Bede, *Historical Works*, trans. J. E. King, Loeb Classical Library. 2 vols (Cambridge, MA: Harvard University Press, 1976), vol. II, p. 383.

3   Jean Leclercq, *The Love of Learning and the Desire for God: A Study of Monastic Culture*, 2nd ed. (New York: Fordham University Press, 1974), page 90.

4   Translation from Simon Keynes and Michael Lapidge, eds, *Alfred the Great* (Harmondsworth: Penguin, 1983), p. 139.

5   See David Hill, *An Atlas of Anglo-Saxon England* (Toronto: University of Toronto Press, 1981), pp. 39–41.

6   Craig Williamson, ed., *The Old English Riddles of the Exeter Book* (Chapel Hill, NC: University of North Carolina Press, 1977), p. 25.

Further Reading

RECENT ESSAY COLLECTIONS

Baker, Peter S., ed. *The Beowulf Reader*. First published as *Beowulf: Basic Readings*. Basic Readings in Anglo-Saxon England 1. New York: Garland, 2000.

Barnhouse, Rebecca, and Benjamin C. Withers, eds. *The Old English Hexateuch: Aspects and Approaches*. Kalamazoo, MI: Medieval Institute Publications, 2000.

Bjork, Robert E., ed. *Cynewulf: Basic Readings*. Basic Readings in Anglo-Saxon England, 4. New York: Garland, 1996.

Bjork, Robert E., and John D. Niles, eds. *A Beowulf Handbook*. Lincoln, NE: University of Nebraska Press, 1997.

Chase, Colin, ed. *The Dating of Beowulf*. Toronto Old English Series, 6. Toronto and Buffalo: Published in association with the Centre for Medieval Studies University of Toronto by University of Toronto Press, 1997.

Damico, Helen, and Alexandra Hennessey Olsen, eds. *New Readings on Women in Old English Literature*. Bloomington: Indiana University Press, 1990.

Fulk, R. D., ed. *Interpretations of "Beowulf": A Critical Anthology*. Bloomington: Indiana University Press, 1991.

Godden, Malcolm, and Michael Lapidge, eds. *The Cambridge Companion to Old English Literature*. Cambridge: Cambridge University Press, 1991.

Lapidge, Michael, John Blair, Simon Keynes, and Donald Scragg, eds. *The Blackwell Encyclopedia of Anglo-Saxon England*. Oxford: Blackwell, 1999.

Liuzza, R. M., ed. *Old English Literature: Critical Essays*. New Haven, CT: Yale University Press, 2002.

Liuzza, R. M., ed. *The Poems of MS Junius 11: Basic Readings*. Basic Readings in Anglo-Saxon England. New York: Routledge, 2002.

O'Keeffe, Katherine O'Brien, ed. *Old English Shorter Poems: Basic Readings*. Basic Readings in Anglo-Saxon England, 3. New York: Garland, 1994.

O'Keeffe, Katherine O'Brien, ed. *Reading Old English Texts*. Cambridge: Cambridge University Press, 1997.
Pulsiano, Phillip, and Elaine Treharne, eds. *A Companion to Anglo-Saxon Literature*. Oxford: Blackwell, 2001.
Reuter, Timothy, ed. *Alfred the Great: Papers from the Eleventh-Centenary Conference*. Studies in Early Medieval Britain, 3. Aldershot: Ashgate, 2003.
Richards, Mary P., ed. *Anglo-Saxon Manuscripts: Basic Readings*. Basic Readings in Anglo-Saxon England, 2. New York: Garland, 1994.
Szarmach, Paul E., ed. *Holy Men and Holy Women: Old English Prose Saints' Lives and their Contexts*. Albany, NY: State University of New York Press, 1996.
Szarmach, Paul E., and Deborah A. Oosterhouse, eds. *Old English Prose: Basic Readings*. Basic Readings in Anglo-Saxon England, 5. New York: Garland, 2000.

TRANSLATIONS

Treharne's *Anthology* has facing-page translations:
Treharne, Elaine, *Old and Middle English c.890–c.1400: An Anthology, Second Edition* (Oxford: Blackwell, 2004).
The two volumes of *English Historical Documents* translate many texts of historical interest, including the *Anglo-Saxon Chronicle*:
Douglas, David C., and George W. Greenaway, eds. *English Historical Documents: 1042–1189*. Vol. 2. New York: Oxford University Press, 1968.
Whitelock, Dorothy, ed. *English Historical Documents: c.500–1042*. 2nd edn. Vol. 1. London: Routledge, 1979.
Translations of *Beowulf* are legion, but for a student's edition of Seamus Heaney's recent verse translation see:
Donoghue, Daniel, ed., and Seamus Heaney, trans. *Beowulf: A Verse Translation*. New York: Norton, 2002.
Other recommended translations:
Bradley, S., trans. *Anglo-Saxon Poetry*. London: Dent, 1982.
Liuzza, R. M., trans. *Beowulf: A New Verse Translation*. Peterborough, Ont.: Broadview, 2000.
Swanton, Michael, trans. *Anglo-Saxon Prose*. London: Dent, 1975.

SCHOLARLY EDITIONS OF WORKS DISCUSSED

Poetry

The separate editions of Old English poems are too numerous to list here, but the standard collection is:

Krapp, G. P., and E. V. K. Dobbie, eds. *The Anglo-Saxon Poetic Records.* 6 vols. New York: Columbia University Press, 1931–53.

Alfred and the prose of his reign

Bately, Janet, ed. *The Old English Orosius.* Oxford: Oxford University Press, 1980.

Miller, Thomas, ed. *The Old English Version of Bede's Ecclesiastical History of the English People.* Reprint. London: Oxford University Press, 1959.

Sedgefield, Walter J., ed. *King Alfred's Old English Version of Boethius De consolatione philosophiae.* Oxford: Clarendon Press, 1899. Reprinted Darmstadt: Wissenschaftlich Buchgesellschaft, 1968.

Sweet, Henry, ed. *King Alfred's West-Saxon Version of Gregory's Pastoral Care.* 2 vols. London: Oxford University Press, 1871. Reprinted Millwood, NY: Kraus, 1988.

Anglo-Saxon Chronicle

Several volumes of *The Anglo-Saxon Chronicle: A Collaborative Edition*, general editors David Dumville and Simon Keynes (Cambridge: Brewer, 1983–) have already appeared, but still useful is:

Plummer, Charles, ed. *Two of the Saxon Chronicle Parallel: With Supplementary Extracts from the Others.* Rev. edn. Oxford: Clarendon Press, 1952.

Translations are also conveniently found in the two volumes of *English Historical Documents* cited above.

Anonymous homilies

Morris, R., ed. *The Blickling Homilies of the Tenth Century.* London: Oxford University Press, 1880. Reprint 1967.

Scragg, D. G., ed. *The Vercelli Homilies and Related Texts.* Oxford: Oxford University Press, 1992.

Ælfric

Clemoes, Peter, ed. *Ælfric's Catholic Homilies: The First Series Text.* Oxford: Oxford University Press, 1997.

Godden, Malcolm, ed. *Ælfric's Catholic Homilies: The Second Series Text.* London: Oxford University Press, 1979.

Godden, Malcolm, ed. *Ælfric's Catholic Homilies: Introduction, Commentary, and Glossary.* Oxford: Oxford University Press, 2000.

Pope, John C., ed. *Homilies of Ælfric: A Supplementary Collection.* 2 vols. London: Oxford University Press, 1967–8.

Skeat, Walter W., ed. *Ælfric's Lives of Saints*. Reprint. 2 vols. London: Oxford University Press, 1966.

Zupitza, Julius, ed. *Ælfrics Grammatik und Glossar*. Berlin: Weidman, 1880. Reprinted with a preface by Helmut Gneuss, 1966.

Wulfstan

Bethurum, Dorothy, ed. *The Homilies of Wulfstan*. Oxford: Clarendon Press, 1957.

Bibliographies

Annual bibliographies are compiled by two journals, *Anglo-Saxon England* and the *Old English Newsletter*. For a comprehensive survey up to 1972 see:

Greenfield, Stanley B., and Fred C. Robinson. *A Bibliography of Publications on Old English Literature to the End of 1972*. Toronto: University of Toronto Press, 1980.

Index

R

Hild 55–7, 59, 69, 74
Hildeburh *see Beowulf*, Hildeburh
history 101
  ages of the world 87–8, 91, 93,
    97–8
  see also Alfredian translations,
    Orosius; *Anglo-Saxon Chronicle*;
    apocalypse; Bede, *Ecclesiastical
    History*
homily 78–98
  definition 84
Hrothgar *see Beowulf*, Hrothgar
Husband's Message 13–15, 23, 48,
  76
Hygd *see Beowulf*, Hygd
Hygelac *see Beowulf*, Hygelac

imminence of the Last Judgment *see*
  apocalypse
Isidore of Seville 93, 100

Jarrow xi, 60, 100
jewelry *see* treasure
Judgment Day *see* apocalypse
Judith 40–2
Juliana 61, 63–4
justice 82–3
  see also court of law; lawcode

Last Judgment *see* apocalypse
Latin ix–x, 47–8, 55, 59–72, 86,
  100–1
lawcode 8–9, 98–9, 106
  Moses as lawgiver 42
Lindisfarne xi, 60
literacy 4, 23, 59–60, 62–5, 104–6
lord/thane relation 10–11, 16–17,
  34–6, 49, 72–4, 79
  see also gift(s); love
love 10–15, 49, 115
Lucifer *see* Satan
lyric xii, 9–13, 47–8

manuscript(s) xii, 124
  capitalization and layout 3,
    45, 54, 57–8, 64, 68, 85,
    105
marriage 8, 10–11, 27–8, 36, 70,
  115–16
Mary 72
metaphor 48, 55, 59, 81, 102–3,
  122–3
Meters of Boethius 109
metonym 29–30, 38
millennium *see* apocalypse
miracle 41, 56–79
  purpose in a saint's life 69
monster(s) *see Beowulf*, dragon;
  Beowulf, Grendel; *Beowulf*,
  Grendel's mother
Moses 42–4, 87

Njal's Saga 8, 37

oath *see* vow
objective correlative 39, 49, 51
Ohthere 111
Olaf Trygvasson 22
oral formula *see* formula
orality ix, 2–9, 14–15, 23, 52,
  56–61, 65, 67, 95–6, 103
Orosius' *Seven Books of History against
  the Pagans see* Alfredian
  translations, Orosius
Orpheus and Eurydice 108
Oswald 66, 71

pagan, heathen ix, xi, 27, 52–3,
  55, 58–9, 61, 67–8, 71,
  80–1, 87–8, 92–7, 110–11,
  116
Paulinus, bishop 30–1
performance 94–6
pilgrimage, *peregrinatio* 81
pledge *see* vow

8365